LOVE LIFE

ALSO BY **ROB LOWE**

Stories I Only Tell My Friends

LOVE LIFE

ROB LOWE

SIMON &
SCHUSTER

London · New York · Sydney · Toronto · New Delhi

A CBS COMPANY

First published in Great Britain by Simon & Schuster UK Ltd, 2014
A CBS COMPANY

1 3 5 7 9 10 8 6 4 2

Simon & Schuster UK Ltd
1st Floor
222 Gray's Inn Road
London WC1X 8HB

www.simonandschuster.co.uk

Simon & Schuster Australia, Sydney
Simon & Schuster India, New Delhi

A CIP catalogue record for this book is available from the British Library

ISBN: 978-1-47113-728-0
ISBN: 978-1-47113-730-3 (ebook)

design by Joy O'Meara
Christopher Lin

The author and publishers have made all reasonable efforts to contact
copyright holders for permission, and apologise for any omissions or errors
in the form of credits given. Corrections may be made to future printings.

Photographs are courtesy
of the author and his family. Film logic: 61 ABCU Photo Bank via Getty Images:
115, 160 (bottom left) Playboy: 156 HBO: 187 (top right);
Showtime 187 (bottom right) Sony Pictures Television: 187 (center);
Getty Images: 243 (right).

Printed and bound by CPI Group (UK) Ltd, Croydon, CR0 4YY

To Lovey

CONTENTS

LOVE LIFE

Characters of Malibu,
Icons of the Valley

I think it was Alfred Hitchcock who said 90 percent of successful moviemaking is in the casting. The same is true in life. Who you are exposed to, who you choose to surround yourself with, is a unique variable in all of our experiences and it is hugely important in making us who we are. Seek out interesting characters, tough adversaries and strong mentors and your life can be rich, textured, highly entertaining and successful, like a Best Picture winner. Surround yourself with dullards, people of vanilla safety and unextraordinary ease, and you may find your life going straight to DVD.

To be fair, early on, we often have less of a say in the casting of our lives. We don't choose our parents or our schools. And that is where we are formed; it is certainly where I learned some fundamental truths. Not the least of which is this:

You never forget the first time you find a woman's vibrator.

My brother Chad and I were rummaging around our pal Danny's tree house–like cottage that he shared with his single mom. I was thirteen; my brother and his friend were around nine. I had taken to co-opting my brother's friends in those early days after our arrival in Malibu because thirteen-year-olds thought boys who wanted to "act" were probably "queer," but nine-year-olds held no judgments about my career aspirations. Chad and I had always been close, bonded by a tumultuous cross-country uprooting and the divorce that instigated it; if he resented my glomming on to his friends, he never showed it.

Chad, Danny and I spent our free time attempting to "shoot" the hill on Larkspur Lane on our skateboards and hiding perishable items among the shelves of our local market, to monitor as they rotted and began to stink. Danny's mom worked at the checkout counter and every boy I knew had a confused, early-adolescent, dim-witted crush on her. With her sandy hair, light eyes and girlish body, it was often hard to reconcile her hippie-dippy, surf-babe looks with the fact that she was our buddy's mother. Long before the term had been invented, she was the original MILF.

One day, sitting on her waterbed with its leopard-print sheets, watching *Gilligan's Island* on a tiny black and white TV, I had rolled over onto a strange, white, missile-shaped device. It began to buzz and vibrate; I began to examine the mysterious obelisk closely.

I don't think any of the three of us knew what it was, but between the location in which it was found, its shape and the sickly expression on Danny's face, there was an unspoken consensus to investigate no further. I daintily hid the thing back under the sheets where I found it and we never spoke of the incident. Lesson: Sometimes it's best to just "move on."

Like so many in the post-Woodstock, pre-AIDS, ERA-and-EST-driven era of midseventies Malibu, Danny's mom was no stranger to countercultural mores. After school one day, as the three of us sat eating her homemade avocado pie, she asked my nine-year-old brother if he wanted to be "smoked out." Chad looked at me with what today would be called a "WTF?" look, having no idea what was being offered to him. We knew that Danny was a cannabis early adopter, but Chad and I were still sons of the Midwest; we were petrified of drugs. So far.

We were in the minority. If there is one thing that a newly transplanted misfit teen doesn't want to be, it's that: standing on the outside of a peer circle. So, after observing the popular kids whipping out their bongs and pipes after a tough day in woodshop or madrigals, I knew what I had to do to ingratiate myself to my fellow thirteen-year-olds. I hopped the bus to Malibu's only record store for a little shopping spree.

I always liked riding the bus. Because I rode them frequently into Hollywood for my auditions, I knew most of the drivers by name. I particularly liked the ones who let my friends and me hang upside down like monkeys from the overhead safety bars, swinging wildly as we sped down the Pacific Coast Highway.

At the record shop, standing in front of the glass case containing the various dope-smoking accouterments, I decided on a tiny, pocket-sized wooden pot pipe, mostly because it looked like one of Captain Kirk's phasers from *Star Trek*. And in truth, over the coming weeks I got more use out of it as a toy, running through the sage-scented gullies and swales of the Malibu hills pretending to be shooting Klingons, than I did using it for its intended purpose. Because my dark secret was that I hated pot.

My "prop" pipe did the trick and I didn't have to smoke at the bus stop in the morning to be cool. I would pull it out of my pocket and brandish it like I was Bob Marley, and eventually the other kids would be too stoned to notice that I never actually used it. I suppose it was an early bit of acting on my part, and it got results; presenting a façade would become a tool I would use to cope with the necessity of "fitting in" (to poor effect) up until my midtwenties.

Malibu in the mid- to late seventies was a breeding ground for many artists who would shape the next decade. There were other young actors to come out of that time and place, and I think it had a lot to do with being surrounded by an unrelenting fusillade of characters and quacks.

This may have been one of the reasons my mother chose Malibu as our new home in the first place. An expatriate from the land of Midwestern, Eisenhower, country-club values, she flourished among the experimental ideas she now found everywhere she turned. My brother and I were unwitting passengers on her lifelong anthropological odyssey.

For example, when my brother was not feeling well, she would accompany him to her favorite doctor. (For reasons I've never understood but am thankful for, my mother rarely involved me in her medical extravaganzas.) The doctor wore corduroy OP shorts and an open-chested Hawaiian shirt. He was suspiciously handsome and insisted that all his patients call him by his first name. His practice was based in a tiny walk-up office a block away from the lone shopping center in town. He had no visible staff. His preferred method of treatment for my brother would be to have him hold various types and sizes of crystals while he manipulated my *mother's* arms, testing her strength in reaction to questions he would ask her about my brother's health.

"Let's see about his gallbladder," he would intone, pressing down on my mom's outstretched arm. If he was able to move it in a way he deemed abnormal, he would pronounce his diagnosis: "Clearly, Chad has an inflamed gallbladder."

The prescription was usually a round of herbal remedies, which he sold us by the boatload. He also often required us to "rent" his crystals for a number of days; we would pay the fee, lug them home for a while and then return them. I have no recollection of them doing anything other than sitting in my mom's study collecting dust.

I didn't judge it then; I judge it even less now. I know of an unbelievably talented A-list actor whose oeuvre runs from drama to comedy to comic book action hero. Like the president of the United States, he is never out of arm's reach of a top secret black briefcase. His daily, hand-chosen battery of exotic (and hugely expensive) crystals provides him with more comfort and power than the launch codes of our nuclear arsenal give to POTUS. Whatever works for you, I suppose.

Although even I have my limits.

People don't realize how banged up you can get making TV and movies. I wouldn't compare it to a tour in Afghanistan, but try taking a full week of all-day riding lessons if you've never been on a horse. Or a three-week crash course of martial arts, grappling and hand-to-hand combat training. Clearly there are more physically demanding jobs in the world, but you often don't expect preparing for a role to kick the shit out of you in the fashion of, say, the professional rodeo. But it can.

After one such character prep, I found myself with some pain in my lower back. As I asked around, the best and the brightest minds of Hollywood kept mentioning the name of the same specialist located in Santa Monica.

"This man is a genius!"

"I had been scheduled for a disk fusion and after four visits, I didn't need surgery!"

I made an appointment.

I almost immediately began to feel uneasy when, once again, the guy had no staff and a cubbyhole office up a flight of stairs. The good doctor looked exactly like the photo double for Fu Manchu, complete with long, wispy, pubic-hair-looking goatee and mustache.

"Take off clothes!" he practically barked at me, pointing to the massage table.

I began to think of all the Hollywood glitterati who had recommended him. Did he frog-march *them* naked to this flimsy table as well? Not yet knowing the great and extremely useful axiom "Just because someone has an Oscar doesn't mean they know anything about anything," I dutifully stripped and dove onto the table.

For the next hour and a half the guy did nothing but move his hands in strange motions over my body. In ninety minutes he never laid a hand on me (I probably should have been grateful)—no massage, chiropractic adjustments, acupuncture needles or any other type of treatment, just his hands relentlessly moving in the air over my back in little circles, like some demented deejay spinning records. Eventually I left in as much pain as I had been in when I arrived, minus two hundred dollars cash.

In this particular era in SoCal, characters and oddballs weren't limited to the medical profession. Local values and customs also made for a great education in human nature.

Among my age group growing up in Malibu, no one was more hated than anyone hailing from the San Fernando Valley. "Valleys," then a pejorative on par with the horrific use of the N-word, was thrown around to describe people who had the audacity to live over the hills in the suburban sprawl of Van Nuys, Encino, Sherman Oaks and Calabasas. Much more traditional, conservative, and working-class than most anyone living on the coast, these kids had to battle for a claim to enjoy Malibu's beaches and surf spots.

The great irony was that the Valley kids, also known as "Kooks," were every bit as good and often better than the locals were at surfing.

Fights would break out on the sand and in the water with equal frequency. I once saw a guy strangling another with his surfboard leash; another time I watched an *Outsiders*-like rumble in the parking lot at Zuma Beach. It looked like a California version of Hitler's Aryan Nation, dressed in board shorts or wetsuits, beating the snot out of each other. This would come in handy later, when I shot a giant teen fracas in my first movie.

When I was old enough to get my learner's permit and began to explore the dangerous and dreaded Kanan Road, which led to the Valley, I found that it wasn't as bad a place as I was led to believe.

I discovered that the blast furnace of San Fernando produced its own landlocked answer to Malibu's would-be stars. At the beach, the hot band to watch was the Surf Punks. In the Valley, the Runaways were trailblazing the path for all-girl bands to come. In auditions around town, I was often coming up on the losing end of Ventura Boulevard phenom Rad Daly. Already a staple of *16 Magazine* and *Tiger Beat*, Rad was the guy you had to beat for every middling sitcom pilot. (At that early point in my career, most of the projects I could land a meeting on were middling at best.) Soon, fellow second-generation performers like Moon Unit and Dweezil Zappa would become as well-known as the Sheen and Penn brothers.

Kids in the Valley had their own vernacular—absolutely no one in Southern California spoke as they did—and when Moon Zappa documented it perfectly in the song "Valley Girl," the entire country co-opted "Grody," "Like, I'm so *sure!*" and the evergreen classic "Gag me with a spoon." Valley girl–speak's cultural importance can (unfortunately) not be overstated. Overnight, perfectly well-educated and articulate kids adopted a faux-bimbo lilt and hair-flopping attitude.

Coming, as it did, at the very moment popular entertainment

culture was beginning its now-total contempt for anything learned or adult, the song "Valley Girl" was the seedling riding the airwaves from which many of today's verbal tics sprung. Linguists now have a term for this dumbed-down singsong lilt: "uptalk." The next time your teenage kid says the word "like" twice in a five-word sentence, you'll know whom to thank.

If Malibu was a bastion of laissez-faire, self-centered, malignant disregard, the San Fernando Valley was a different ecosystem entirely. Families still had some semblance of the traditional Protestant values left over from their dust bowl, post–World War II kin who had settled the place. Or think of it this way: In the decade from 1976 to 1986 Tom Joad's kids were the parents in the Valley. In Malibu, it was Hunter S. Thompson.

But there were plenty of lessons of a different sort to be learned from the kids of Ventura Boulevard.

In my peer group from Malibu, although some families were very successful in show business, it would be a few years before the young generation took the baton. Not so in the Valley, and so I got that valuable shot in the arm that any young dreamer needs; I took comfort in seeing that I was not alone. I ran into (and sometimes up against) Moosie Drier of *Oh, God!* and *The Bob Newhart Show* fame. And Kim Richards, the go-to cute little blond girl from all the Disney movies. There was Jennifer McAllister, a talented actress who was doing movies like *Sybil* and who appeared to be the next Jodie Foster, who was also in the mix, already an institution from movies like *Taxi Driver* and *Bugsy Malone*.

The royal family of the Valley was, without question, the Van Pattens. The patriarch, Dick Van Patten, was the star of *Eight Is Enough*, one of the biggest shows on TV, and had an army of great-looking sons and cousins who were always competing at a high level in sports and entertainment.

LOVE LIFE

As you can see below, in the late 1970s there was another version of Camelot, just off Ventura Boulevard.

Kennedys vs. Van Pattens

Powerful Patriarch	Joe Sr. ruthlessly engineered his son's domination of politics in the fifties and sixties	Dick jovially engineered his son's domination of television in the seventies and eighties
Patriarch High-water Mark	Joe Sr. served as ambassador to Great Britain from 1937 to 1940	Dick starred as Tom Bradford in *Eight Is Enough* from 1977 to 1981
The Golden Sons	Joe Jr., Bobby and Jack	Nels, Jimmy and Vince
The Proving Ground	Touch football on the lawn	Tug-of-war on *Battle of the Network Stars*
Son's Finest Moment	JFK upsets Nixon, 1960	Vince upsets John McEnroe, 1981
Female Conquests	Marilyn Monroe	Farrah Fawcett Majors
Family Compound	Hyannis Port, Cape Cod	Patten Place apartment building, Sherman Oaks
Whom They Feared	The Teamsters	The ACNielsen Company

To a scrub like me, this seemed like an impenetrable show business/sports/girl-chasing dynasty. I seem to recall losing a role or two to one of the clan in the early days, possibly the role of "Salami" in *The White Shadow*, which went to Timothy Van Patten. And a few years later, as I got my act together in terms of girls, I would diligently court a gal only to see her drive by in Vince Van Patten's convertible. You can never truly understand the power that a little fame, achievement and good looks can have until you see it up close, and it was very clear to me what side I wanted to be on.

Eventually, I ended up spending a fair amount of time at Patten Place, the large group of apartments Dick owned on Riverside Avenue in the heart of the Valley. It was an early version of what the Oakwood Apartments are today: a safe, clean harbor for struggling actors and the odd, dubious hanger-on. After he beat me out for the part of "the new kid" on *Eight Is Enough* late in its run, Ralph Macchio and I became close on my first movie, *The Outsiders*. Ralph lived in Patten Place, next door to "the Nike Man," a *Tiger Beat* talent scout who seemed to have an endless free supply of the latest Nike wear and who gave it away to any handsome teenage boy he ran across. He also had an obsession with the talk show host John Davidson, whose shows he watched repeatedly on an early-era Betamax.

The Nike man was one of the first people I encountered who made their living around the edges of show business but who weren't actually *in* show business. It may have been the first and certainly not the last time I saw that not everyone got into show business from artistic passion.

The Valley also had a monopoly on actors who were tremendous and tough athletes. In Malibu, the only sports you could expect anyone to participate in were surfing and volleyball. My tastes were more traditional and if I wanted a vigorous game of hoops or football, I would have much better luck on the other side of the hill.

The godfather of show business athletics in the Valley was the king of television, auteur Garry Marshall. He hosted a notoriously elite, every-weekend basketball tournament at his Tarzana home. As the creator of *Happy Days, Laverne and Shirley* and *Mork and Mindy*, he had a very deep bench to draw from. I was thrilled to be included once or twice, with mixed results. Believe me, there is nothing more demoralizing than being dunked over by Lenny and Squiggy or the Fonz.

But Garry was also a great early supporter of my acting career. After many auditions for his series, in early 1980, he cast me in a pilot for his next big TV show, *Mean Jeans*. Unfortunately, the title was the only thing funny about this sitcom set in a hip designer jeans shop. When the Pointer Sisters agreed to sing the title song, I thought I was going to be in a hit. I was wrong. The show never made it to air, sparing the nation the experience of me as a teenage, woman-crazy tailor named Tucker Toomey.

Garry Marshall's benevolence extended far and wide. With his empire, he was able to give first breaks to many, including a pretty blond Valley girl from Taft high who dreamed of being a makeup artist but had no experience. Garry gave her her first job. Many years later I met this now-top-makeup-artist on *Bad Influence* and married her. Garry was the first person invited to my wedding with Sheryl.

The Valley is rimmed on its southern side by the storied Mulholland Drive. High atop the hills, it snakes its way through hairpin turns, romantic lookouts and breathtaking vistas of city lights. But more importantly to me, it was the address of the biggest icons of my youth: Jack Nicholson, Marlon Brando and Warren Beatty. They were everything I aspired to be: authentic artists, titans of their time, while being time*less* and known for a wild streak that made them cool and a little dangerous. When Nicholson's *One Flew over the Cuckoo's Nest* came out, I saw it twelve times. I then went back once more, smuggling in a tape recorder, so I could listen to it whenever I wanted. When Magic Johnson came to the Lakers in 1979, I sat in the nosebleeds to see him and saw Jack sitting courtside. "How cool," I thought. A few years later, when I had some success of my own, I bought Lakers floor seats, directly across from Jack.

When *Heaven Can Wait* came out, I took the bus into Westwood to see it opening weekend at the Mann National Theater, the same theater that would eventually premiere my first movie, *The Outsiders*. Warren Beatty's costar was Dyan Cannon, whose daughter, Jennifer, I would very briefly date. Even as a teenager, being a young actor on the LA dating scene would eventually put you in a direct or indirect competition with the master Hollywood ladies' man.

Warren's reach and domination was so profound, even Jack Nicholson called him "the Pro." He lived in a notoriously cool pad on a shaded turn of Mulholland that always reminded me of the secret entrance the Batmobile used on *Batman*. And, like the caped crusader, Warren owned the night and pretty much anything else he wanted. By the time I was getting a foothold with my first starring roles, he was the embodiment of what a former matinee idol could achieve: from pretty to profound, with his brainy, socially significant *Reds* dominating the Oscars that year.

I had been dating a young, successful actress whom Warren had befriended. To her credit, whenever she was invited "up to Warren's," she would ask me to join. In my stupidity, I always said no. Even a day with my hero couldn't get me into the sweatbox of the Valley when all my pals were hitting the beach in Malibu.

But one night I made an exception.

I hopped into my girlfriend's two-seater and began to climb to the top of the Hollywood Hills. Mulholland Drive, named after William Mulholland, the visionary engineer who figured out how to bring in the water that built modern LA, led me past Jack Nicholson's house and I instantly thought of his masterpiece *Chinatown*, about the intrigue of getting the water that built modern LA. Soon we arrived at a set of chic, modern gates. Inside, the driveway rose even higher to the top of the most scenic spot of the Valley's southern rim. We parked in the motor court of a sleek, contemporary, white one-story home. "Understated glamour" would be the best description of its style.

Warren met us at the door. I had never met him in person but had spoken to him a few times when he would call my girlfriend. He was always charming and welcoming. At one point he gave me the low-down on my soon-to-be leading lady in the movie *Class*, Jacqueline Bisset. ("She's a champ," he said.)

"Oh, hey, come on in," he said, welcoming us into an almost totally empty living room. "I, uh, I'm so sorry it's so bare. I've had a couple of years away at work and haven't really furnished much."

I knew he was referring to the legendary and famously long shooting of *Reds* and I noted his unassuming understatement. Scanning the room, I did notice one furnishing: his Oscar for Best Director for *Reds* sitting on the otherwise empty mantel.

Oscars are everything you would imagine them to be. To see a real one in the flesh, for an actor, is to see the crown jewels. It's the most recognized and coveted totem in the world. (An Amazon aboriginal would know an Academy Award on sight but not a Nobel Prize.) They are both easy to hold and extraordinarily heavy. Warren's Oscar was glinting and new, unlike the first one I had seen a few years earlier on a debauched late-night rendezvous with an actress who had won years earlier. Sitting on her TV in a tiny apartment in the flats of Hollywood, hers was worn and corroded, with specs of green in its creases.

Watching Warren pad around his house, I was struck with the thought that he looked exactly like Warren Beatty. If you have ever met a star in the flesh, you know it goes one of two ways: They look so good they're almost like impersonators of themselves, or you think, "Oy! What happened to them?"

"I have two Burt Reynolds movies for us in the screening room," said Warren, leading us down a flight of stairs to a setup that had a theater-size screen, rows of comfy couches and almost unbearably romantic mood lighting. He was padding around barefoot, in jeans and a crisp white shirt; the whole scene would have made Mother Teresa want to bang him.

Warren's date for the night was an actress I recognized as a semi-regular on *WKRP in Cincinnati*. She sat to his left, with me on his right. Warren picked up a phone built into the arm of the couch and asked the projectionist to start the movie.

"I think we'll watch *Stick* first."

I had always been fascinated with what movie stars felt about one another. Were they supportive? Jealous? Did they take notes and learn from each other? As the movie began, I was curious what, if anything, Warren would say about it. After all, at that moment, he was the undisputed king of Hollywood. The movie started.

"Hmm," mumbled Warren.

"Oh, I see," he said to no one in particular.

"Ahh." He smiled to himself.

Halfway through the movie, my curiosity got the best of me.

"What do you think?" I asked him.

"Very interesting. He's using a lot of long lenses," Warren replied sagely.

I tried to comprehend how he could look at the scene and know what kind of lens it was shot with. I wondered what he was seeing to recognize these technical details so easily. It made me realize that I had a tremendous amount to learn about moviemaking.

Meanwhile, the girl from *WKRP* was getting restless.

"Is there any ice cream?" she asked, clearly not as enthralled with Burt or dissecting what equipment he was using on-screen. "I'm *starving*."

Warren and the girls immediately disembarked for the kitchen. Like an idiot, I stayed in the screening room watching the movie.

After a while, it became clear they weren't coming back. I made my way up to the kitchen to find them. I came upon them each eating directly out of containers of Häagen-Dazs. They seemed to become immediately quiet as I entered, but Warren was as gracious as ever.

"We were just talking about you," he said, offering up his pralines and cream to me.

I looked at my girlfriend, who was scrunched up next to WKRP, looking like the cat that ate the canary.

"You remind me *so* much of Warren," said WKRP. It was a great compliment, and standing right next to him I felt my color rise.

"It's true," he said. "I started young like you and was dating an actress more famous than I was, just like you."

"Natalie Wood?" asked my girlfriend, glowing with pride from the comparison.

"Exactly," answered Warren. "She was a big deal and I wasn't, but I had a huge movie about to come out in *Splendor in the Grass* and I knew my life was going to change. Like you, Rob, when *The Outsiders* comes out."

"Well, I hope you're right," I said, realizing that ice cream had never tasted so good. I looked at the clock on the wall and thought, "I'm eighteen years old, it's midnight at Warren Beatty's house and I'm having dessert while he talks about my future."

"You remind me of Natalie Wood," he remarked casually to my girlfriend. I remember thinking, "*There* it is. The lay-down hand. The line that would turn any young actress into his personal concubine for life."

"It's funny," he said, continuing. "Natalie was always getting asked by Frank Sinatra to come up to his house and lay by the pool. I never paid much attention to it, but years later, just a few years before

Natalie died, I asked her, 'Hey, we're both adults now, what exactly were you doing all those days at Sinatra's?' And she looked me right in the eyes and said, 'Oh, Warren, what do you think we were doing? We were fucking!' Isn't that funny?" He smiled at me, shaking his head at the memory.

I looked over at my girlfriend, who looked away, ashen faced. And the penny dropped.

Thanks for the heads-up, Warren Beatty. You're my hero to this day.

Chad and I, around the time we arrived in Malibu.

Matthew Applies to College

My son Matthew is eighteen. When I look at him, I often don't recognize any part of the little boy I have loved for so long. Sometimes I do; I'll see a fleeting expression or the light will catch him in a manner that for a moment makes him look as he once was. With his size-thirteen feet and his mother's long limbs, he can still look like a young colt navigating an open field. He has my love of history and politics, my interest in factoids, trivia and obscure information, most of it of limited interest to anyone else. Unlike me, Matthew is content to let you come to him, confident in his silences. He auditions for no one.

We've always been close, but I have come to realize our relationship has been predicated on proximity. We've loved reading together from the time he was a baby; we explored the hills and beaches and railroad tracks of our neighborhood. We ran in the yard with our dogs; we navigated the laughter, love and hurt of adolescence together. Soon the geography of our relationship will change and we will build a new one based around distance, and while I hope it will be as close as before, I know it will never be the same.

Matthew is in the middle of the college application process. Choosing a school has always been an arduous and drama-filled travail for our family. I have only recently recovered from the great kindergarten search. After gaining a coveted meeting with a prestigious school's admissions director, I watched my son jam a shark's tooth into the woman's ear. Why a supposedly learned child-care expert would have such a small health hazard within a child's reach remains a mystery and should have been a sign that perhaps this fancy-pants school wasn't all it was cracked up to be. There were other signs that I chose to ignore as well.

While some of the school's third and fourth graders carried books through the hallways, a larger portion carried skateboards. Having grown up in Malibu, I was not unaccustomed to Southern California's less-than-respectful fashion ethos, but even I was taken aback by the sheer numbers of boys dressed like Jeff Spicoli. When we were touring a sixth-grade science class, a kid raised his hand with a question. "Pete," the eleven-year-old student asked the teacher, who was in his midforties and wearing surf shorts, "what is more common, zooplankton or phytoplankton?" While I struggled to come up with the answer myself, I struggled even more with the concept of a little boy referring to his adult teacher by his first name. I was well versed in this sort of educational culture; in fact, my mother had placed my younger brother Micah in such a kindergarten in Malibu years ago, a local institution. The founder of the school didn't believe in "structured" teaching or apparently discipline of any kind. Whenever I picked my brother up from school, many kids were AWOL, running around in the hills above the school like savages. Even as a sixteen-year-old I had the notion that this was no way to run a railroad, so, years later, I was sort of relieved when Matthew took matters into his own hands and ended our application process with the shark's tooth.

My wife, Sheryl, and I did eventually find the right school for him. I think we all react to the way we were raised as we try to navigate our roles as parents. Neither my mother nor my father was particularly involved in my life at school (although they did instill a work ethic and made sure all homework was done). With my own kids, I wanted to be as much a part of their school experience as I could, as did Sheryl.

For me, this meant taking part in as many school functions and extracurricular activities as I could. I coached both of my sons' elementary school basketball teams. One of my fondest memories is winning the league championship for the school's first time. (As Ty Cobb said, "it ain't bragging if you've done it.") Even though some of what I thought were my best motivation techniques were probably too advanced for sixth graders, I loved being with the kids. I'm not sure if they fully appreciated my grabbing them by the jerseys at half time, eyes blazing, and admonishing them with, "No one, and I mean *no one*, comes into our house and pushes us around!" When the kids looked at me with blank faces, I would tell them, "It's from the film *Rudy*. You know, Ara Parseghian? The great Notre Dame coach? . . . Ah, never mind, just toughen up out there!" And you know what? Inevitably, they would.

I learned that kids are like actors on a set: They want to know that their director gives a shit, has an actual plan and, just maybe, knows what he's doing. In other words, they want leadership. And you can't attempt to lead by being all things to all people or a slave to PC society—which brings me to why I was eventually overthrown as the basketball coach in a parent-led coup d'état and why they've never won a championship since.

Lots of kids wanted to play basketball in that sixth-grade class. I suggested that rather than having one huge team on which some kids would inevitably not get much playing time, we field two teams, with two different coaches, so the greatest number of kids could play. I then went through almost Manhattan Project–like analytics to ensure both teams were equally matched. But after my first few practices, I began to sense trouble.

A gaggle of moms had been eyeballing me throughout our first scrimmage game with the grade's other team. It soon became clear that they were not fans of my methods.

"Why didn't my son play very much?" asked the ringleader with the same righteous fire as Norma Rae. I couldn't very well tell her that her boy had no interest in learning the fundamentals of basketball or playing basketball, and certainly not winning at basketball.

"We're all just getting our footing out there. The more they learn, the more they'll play. But your boy's working hard," I lied, and immediately hated myself.

Then the next mom spoke up. "I don't see why you are dividing these boys' friendships by letting your team win. These teams are from the same class!"

"You . . . You don't want anyone to win?" I responded. I had heard about this new mind-set about sports in schools, but thought it was only a BS punch line for late-night talk show monologues.

"Well, I certainly don't think you should be *keeping score!*" she answered. The other moms nodded gravely.

I explained that, in my view, the tradition of noting the amount of baskets achieved, adding them up and comparing the total to the other team's is the only objective method to see who played better. The moms sniffed and looked at one another. I haven't felt such tension and disapproval since I sang with Snow White at the Oscars.

"Well," Norma Rae said with finality, "I don't think it's fair to have winners and losers."

I thought about debating that point. In my estimation, there is no more virulent motivator in life than wanting to win.

As the season progressed, so did our team. We practiced hard, but always with an element of fun. Still, I could see that there was a type of parent who didn't want to have their kids do push-ups if they goofed off, or run laps if they were late, or get benched for a lack of motivation.

I loved these boys and loved coaching them. Telling a shy, awkward kid that he "can do this" when he clearly thinks he can't, and has probably never been told he can, would almost move me to tears. When that kid made his only basket of the entire season, in our league championship, I wanted to run out and hug him. Instead, I gave him the game ball.

After winning the championship, I found out that there were no awards (or anything else) to memorialize the boys' achievement, so I decided to buy each kid a small trophy myself. I had it inscribed with the school's name, the year and the word "champions." I soon heard from the school's PE teacher that he'd been getting complaints from parents whose kids didn't win the tournament and so would not be getting a trophy. Furthermore, I was told that the kids would not be allowed to attend the awards/pizza dinner I'd arranged unless I got trophies for the other school team as well.

"Does anyone object to the winning team's trophy showing that they were, in fact, the winning team?" I asked.

"Honestly; yes. But if *all* the kids got the same style and size trophy, I think you could get away with it."

"Okay. Do you want me to pay for these additional trophies?"

"Yes. That would be great."

"What about the other coach?" I asked. I was happy to foot the bill but curious as to where the other team's leader was in all of this nonsense.

"Oh, he says he's done with the season."

I held our awards dinner at our local pizza parlor, setting up an awards table on top of the Ms. Pac-Man machine. As I handed out the Golden Basketball Man to each kid, the television above us showed the Oscars being handed out down in LA. The pizza parlor was decidedly more fun and fulfilling. A few weeks later I was informed of a new school policy: Parents would no longer be permitted to participate in after-school athletic programs. This was probably as it should have been in the first place. The next year local college volunteers were brought in. I watched and rooted as an incredibly sweet and well-meaning young lady tried to figure out what a three-second violation was and how to inbound the ball correctly. Turns out she'd never played basketball; her expertise was water polo. The team went two for twelve that year.

Sometimes at pickup, waiting for my boys to get out of class, I would see my old team on the playground. We'd play a little horse. I'd teach them the Xs and Os, the fundamentals of the pick and roll, but they showed me something, too. From them I learned (or relearned) how important adolescent friendships are, how impressionable young boys can be and how much male, adult attention means to their development. I learned that they rise to a challenge, crave it and desperately want a responsibility they can meet. I saw their humble appreciation of being recognized for a job well done. And I realized that maybe that's all anyone really wants, including me.

When Matthew finally opens the college-acceptance letter that we all prayed would come, I know it will be the beginning of his life without us. This is almost too much for me to contemplate. I prefer to live in denial that my relationship with him will be irrevocably changed.

Instead I goad myself into focusing on the bright side of having my beloved firstborn leaving home, of having the empty bedroom full of his boyhood touchstones, the sudden quiet when his incessant techno dubstep electronic dance music no longer blasts through the floorboards down into my office as I try to read a script and maintain my sanity. Yes, instead I think about the amazing! fantastic! wonderful! gifts that will come from being completely cut off from his daily life and academic experience.

And those would be what, exactly? First and foremost: No more field trips to chaperone!

My wife, Sheryl, once volunteered me to chaperone my son's third-grade class on a weekend trip to SeaWorld in San Diego, making Matthew and me captives in a six-hour van ride with a parent we barely knew.

In spite of being professionally gregarious, in my nonpaid hours I'm a bit of a hermit. After being around a crew of fifty people for twelve hours a day on a film set, I really like my alone time and as always I abhor small talk. I love to delve into subjects one doesn't in polite conversation, but idle banter, after about ten minutes, makes me wish I was still guzzling kamikazes at the Hard Rock Café. Or, in severe cases, leads me to consider reenacting John Gielgud's warm-bathtub wrist-slicing suicide scene in *Caligula*.

The van ride would provide lots of time to get acquainted with the other class dad. The boys sat in the back doing their thing. I was riding shotgun in what reminded me of Scooby-Doo's Mystery Machine, but without the charming paint job.

Things went south quickly.

I had become suspicious of a Styrofoam cooler in the foot well between our seats and eventually the dad noticed.

"Help yourself to a cold one," he said, opening the lid to reveal that it was packed with bottles of Budweiser.

Now, I'm not a lawyer, but I often play one on television, and I think I know enough about California law to be squeamish about having an open container of booze in the car.

I spent the rest of the drive on alert to his opening one for himself, but he never did. He must have been saving them for his tour of Sea-World. Soon we were driving through the heart of Los Angeles, down the 405, the busiest freeway in the country.

"What do they call this city?" he asked, looking around in wonder.

"Um, Westwood," I replied, trying not to pass a judgment on him for asking that question when he'd just finished telling me he had lived in Southern California his whole life.

"So, this would be LA, then?" he asked.

"Yes. That is correct. We are passing through LA," I answered. I thought, "Maybe I should have a beer."

Later, at SeaWorld we met up with the other parents and kids and took our tour, which all the kids loved. Soon it was nighttime.

One of the dirty little secrets about having lived three-quarters of my life in show business is that I have developed a stress-reducing mechanism of only focusing on the matter directly at hand. This is great for navigating the uncontrollable uncertainty of life on film sets but probably not ideal for life in the real world. And so it slowly dawned on me that I hadn't fully comprehended the reality of that night's sleeping accommodations. I'm not a complete idiot; I knew I'd be participating in, and had packed for, a campout at Sea-World. But I did not realize that we would be sleeping inside the manatee exhibit.

My traveling companion, now happily drinking his Bud, told me that this was a rare treat—SeaWorld offered this only to select schools. He then grabbed his son and bolted into the exhibit to "get a good spot to sleep."

The manatee exhibit is an enormous tank/ecosystem with a

crowded observation area and an underwater viewing area. The place is usually jam-packed with spectators, reminiscent of center court at Flushing Meadows. The elephant-like creatures float around lazily and sometimes stick their walrus faces out of the water for a slightly disturbing stare-down. But that night, as the park closed down, even the manatees were looking to get some shut-eye.

My son and I entered a bunkerlike space under the grandstands. The air was thick and humid, oppressive to the lungs and cold. There were cement walls on three sides. On the fourth wall, we could clearly see the beautiful beasts swimming, in what seemed like slow motion. Apparently, ours was not the only school to be allowed this aquatic backstage pass; the place was infested with screaming, scrambling kids, several of whom, from the sound of their hacking, had debilitating head colds. Through their screeching, I could barely hear my son ask, "Where do we sleep, Dad?" I looked around. The parents and kids had staked out their areas, spreading out their sleeping bags. The floor was tough, hard industrial carpet over cement. I picked a spot in the corner away from the glass tank wall, figuring (correctly, as it turned out) that the light illuminating the tank was on for a reason and would stay that way through the night. I'm not a hothouse flower; I camp often and am not the type to bring air mattresses. I have also camped in the dead of winter. But this was different because I was surrounded by elements I could not control that would in all likelihood *disturb my sleep*. And know this about me: I. Like. My. Sleep. It probably is some sort of post-traumatic stress disorder left over from surviving the decade of the 1980s, where no self-respecting person *ever* slept. As I unrolled our matching Timberland sleeping bags, I hoped against hope that I could find a way to fall asleep among the hacking, yammering kids, floodlights from the tank illuminating the cold cement floor and gentle thumps of manatees banging against the glass.

I snuggled my boy up next to me (he was having a blast) and shut my eyes.

"Hi! Hi there! Rob, right?"

My eyes snapped open to see a mom dragging two kids behind her toward our little campsite.

"Hi! Hi! Hope you don't mind, you seem to have *such* a great spot!" she said, unloading what looked like a week's worth of supplies right next to me. "Box juice? Box juice?" she offered.

"No thanks, I'm just turning in for the night."

"Cool. No problem. Someone said you were here and I didn't believe them. I was like, what would Rob fucking Lowe be doing at SeaWorld?!"

My son, who always appreciates the proper usage of a good piece of profanity, said, "My dad's our chaperone!"

"Ooooh, he looks just like you!" she said, staring at him like he was a puppy in a pet shop window.

It was a rough night. I had a disturbing dream. In order to pay the bills, I was forced to star in a direct-to-DVD sequel to *Free Willy*, but with manatees instead. The plot centered around an emasculated dad (played by me) going through a divorce from his übersuccessful, highly strung wife (played by Sarah Jessica Parker, although at some point it was also the actress from *Footloose*—you know how dreams are). Our adopted Sudanese son took comfort and mentorship from a handsome whale specialist at the local aquarium (Scott Bakula, I think) and helped him save a sick sea elephant. After our marriage counselor (Paul Giamatti) fell into the tank during a "family healing day," he was saved by the manatee and so was our marriage.

At some point, I awoke, startled, heart racing. I was relieved, just as I am when I awake from other recurring nightmares, of unwittingly drinking a fifth of alcohol or giving a speech while my teeth fall out.

I rolled over, trying to get comfortable on the cold, rigid floor,

among the chorus of adult snoring and juvenile sniffling and cough-
ing. The light from the manatee tank illuminated the room as if it
were noon instead of three forty-five A.M.

My neighbor, the talky mom, was also wide-awake. And staring
at me. I smiled uncomfortably. She kept staring, unblinking. I had a
passing thought that she might, in fact, be no longer living.

"You don't even remember me, do you?" she said in a flat, robot-
like monotone that managed to convey an element of accusation and
craziness. "We met. Before," she said finally, without offering any
additional information.

I meet a lot of people, doing what I do, and as a single guy in his
teens and twenties who starred in movies and traveled the world, I
made a number of acquaintances, many romantic, most wonderful,
and a few quite bat-shit dangerous and malignant. I chose my words
carefully.

"I'm so sorry, forgive me, where did we meet?"

"The Sunspot," she said, naming a horrific old-school nightclub
on the Pacific Coast Highway that has been closed for over a decade.
I had only been there once, in my wild phase, and my only recollection of the evening was a police car plowing at full speed into a row
of parked cars and ensuing ambulances.

"Oh, yeah. Sure. Sure, right!" I offered with feigned dawning rec-
ognition, calculating that acknowledgment would be the safest and
most polite response. (There are people and a number of actors who
can pull off the blunt and unrepentantly honest "I'm sorry, I have no
idea who you are," but I am not one of them.)

This seemed to break her trance and soon the whole *Fatal Attrac-
tion* vibe had passed, and she returned to being just another parent
surrounded by elementary school kids sleeping in a manatee exhibit.

"Well, good to see you again," she said.

"You too."

"Good night."

The rest of the field trip was uneventful but fun; Matthew and I begged off returning in the Scooby-Doo van and took the train instead.

It is a wonder, what we remember. Small, seemingly forgettable details feel like present, hard-edged objects you could actually hold in your hands; major events go lost until jarred out of unconsciousness by a song or smell or getting reacquainted with an old friend. I remember that field trip. I can't remember my sons' voices as little boys. Time, unfolding in all of its mystery, moving both fast and slow, has made its edit. Some of the things that have fallen away, I try to remember as I hold on to my memories of Matthew as a child. Before they are replaced by those of him as an adult. Before he heads away.

There is a movie called *My Dog Skip*, starring my *Outsiders* costar Diane Lane. I do not recommend it. If you have a child, particularly one about to leave home, watching this film is to be emotionally waterboarded. The story follows a little boy through young adulthood through the eyes of his beloved Jack Russell terrier. It is a great, yet admittedly manipulative, meditation on family, youth and mortality, and I defy you to watch its ending sequence and not have to be medevaced out of your present location.

The boy, now a young man, prepares to go away to school and he worries about his childhood best friend, Skip, now so old and arthritic that he can no longer jump up onto his bed. The boy leaves home; the Jack Russell sits in the boy's room waiting for his return. In the middle of the boy's freshman year, Skip dies. The boy's parents bury him wrapped in his master's Little League jacket.

My son Matthew's beloved dog is a Jack Russell. His name is

Buster. Matthew picked him as a puppy, when he was tiny himself. They sleep together to this day under Matthew's down comforter. The vet has told us that Buster has arthritis now and soon might need to be carried up our stairs. Matthew has asked me to do this for him while he is away at school.

"Will you take care of him for me, Dad?" he asks me one day, not long after we've returned from our college tour, greeted by Buster's howling.

"Of course."

I catch Sheryl's eye but look away. We've both been preparing ourselves in our own ways for this new phase, and both of us are struggling.

"Thanks, Dad," Matthew says, scooping Buster into his arms and heading up to his bedroom.

They take the stairs together, Matthew tucking his dog into the chest of one of my old shirts he's now grown into. I watch him stride away, confident and happy. As I listen closely I can hear him talking to Buster.

"You are my good boy. And I'm going to miss you."

With Matthew and his classmates, camping out among the manatees.

Matthew and his beloved Buster.

Film Acting School

I kissed a man recently, and with romantic intent.

I liked and admired him very much, and professionally he is as good as anyone in his field, but truth be told he isn't conventionally attractive. In fact, he is not tall, lacks any hair whatsoever and is a bit older than anyone I would likely be interested in kissing, regardless of gender.

But I did it anyway, and not without the apprehension you would expect from someone completely new to that sort of thing. I wondered what my wife would think. Since I was being paid for it, I figured she'd be okay with it. And considering the circumstances, I took solace in knowing she wouldn't be asking me, "How long has this been going on?" or "Do you love him?"

Before you start wondering if I'm having one of those sexual identity crises you hear about on daytime chat shows, relax. There are moments that arise in my profession that put you in unexpected and uncharted waters. For me, kissing Evan Handler as Eddie Nero on *Californication* was one of them.

Evan and I had worked together before, on *The West Wing*. I think he played a campaign strategist for Bartlet's reelection. He too has written books, and we bonded over our appreciation for a good memoir and said our traditional actor's good-byes: "Loved working with you. Let's do it again soon!"

I never imagined that when we did, we would be doing a big kiss that would make *A Place in the Sun*'s Elizabeth Taylor and Montgomery Clift proud (Clift more so, probably).

Californication, the brilliant David Duchovny vehicle for Showtime, is the perfect example of a great actor (David) getting a part that is right in his wheelhouse. Like him, the show is subversive and smart as hell. And, like all cable shows, unrelentingly provocative. Hence my first screen kiss with a man. The fact that neither of our characters is gay makes it more so.

I play a delusional, drug-addled, pretentious, sexually carnivorous, Academy Award–winning movie star. I am not unfamiliar with the type. Although I bear a passing resemblance to at least two well-known (and fantastic) actors in my Eddie Nero "look" whom I will not name for fear of reprisal, I based the character on a mix of people. I was able to send up every pretentious contrivance of the archetypal "Method movie star."

It's written to be a show-stopping part, the kind that steals a movie with four scenes or pumps excitement into a series in midrun. Eddie has a number of great speeches, the kind actors kill for.

At a certain point, if you want to make a name for yourself in this business you gotta figure out your "Monkey Trick," as a fellow actor once told me. Some actors specialize in shooting weapons and punching people. Some have the market on playing buffoons cornered, others specialize in roles that require heavy makeup or outrageous wardrobe. Some trade exclusively in a post-ironic blasé attitude. Others choose the opposite tack, taking big (and oftentimes over-the-top) swings. Everyone who is anyone has a Monkey Trick. Among mine is playing people who can speak in large blocks of dialogue and being unafraid of "going for it" in character parts.

Actors are like horses; some of us are better over long distances, some in a sprint, some for kiddie rides and some for dangerous stunt work. Like horses, there are probably some of us who should not leave the barn and probably some who should be "put down."

I was working on two other TV series (*Brothers & Sisters* and *Parks and Recreation*) at the same time when the part came my way. Arnold Schwarzenegger once told me, "My agents never get me parts. I get them for myself or they come some other way." True to the movie legend's word, this part came to me from the guy who cuts my hair.

Duchovny and I share the same hairdresser; they were talking about who could play this bizarre role and my name came up. "I'll call him now," said my guy, Daniel Erdman. On another track, the show's producers called my agents, who said I was unavailable. And in the end, it did take my agents to get both ABC and NBC to let me go work for Showtime. But the lesson here is never leave everything to the experts. Everyone needs oversight.

It's funny what actors take issue with. Some won't do parts where animals are in jeopardy; some won't ever play anyone remotely unlikable—heroes only, please. Some won't do violence. I have no such qualms. This part had man-on-man kissing, but what really made it stand out was some of the most jaw-droppingly explicit language I had ever read.

In my last book I quoted verbatim my favorite speech from *The West Wing*. I won't be doing that here for *Californication*. Kids may be reading this. But trust me when I tell you it was outrageous and not for the faint of heart. Which is why I was interested. You see, I don't confuse who I play with who I am. The minute you start making calculations about what people will think of you as a person based on your work as an actor, you're on the road to becoming a bad one. It is the death of diversity, range and surprise—all of the things I value in someone's body of work. If you are worried about what people think of you, you should go into politics. Real actors take chances.

When Steven Soderbergh asked me to do *Behind the Candelabra*, I hadn't yet read the script but I knew enough to know the things I needed to know: Michael Douglas was playing Liberace, Matt Damon his doe-eyed, innocent boy toy; it was being directed by a master and written by Richard LaGravenese, one of the great screenwriters. So sight-unseen, I was inclined to say yes, unless of course I read the script and my character was blowing a donkey. And given the subject matter, I suppose that may have been a possibility!

As I suspected, the role was terrific. While not huge in screen time, I could see it having a big impact if done in an original, outrageous way. When you are the lead in a picture (as the old-timers would say), you have the luxury of time on camera to inexorably make your mark. In a supporting role or particularly in a cameo, you have to shorten the field. You need to swing at the first pitch and try to crush it, pronto. But you mustn't be showy or unduly attention seeking. It's not your movie. You are a guest and you need to fit in seamlessly. If you can pull off both of these competing techniques, you might just steal a movie or two. I believe all great actors should be able to do both, and my personal favorites have. They are memorable in parts of all sizes; they've been number one on the "call sheet" (where they list the actors according to the size of their role) and number twelve or thirteen.

After a lot of thought, and with the help of an extraordinary team, I had a very special "look" designed for my character, a seventies-era LA Dr. Feelgood. I based it on some of the guys I used to see at Lakers games, back in the day. When I walked on set the first time, both Matt Damon and Michael Douglas burst out laughing. Later, when shooting, Damon was often unable to look me in the eye.

Their extraordinary work made *Behind the Candelabra* the most critically acclaimed and highest-rated movie in the history of HBO. It was nominated for every possible award and it earned me my fifth Golden Globe nomination. And although I had only five or six scenes, I truly had never gotten that kind of obsessed, positive feedback from anything I had done before. My face, as Dr. Jack Startz, was everywhere, and people still ask me about that role.

I followed that performance with JFK in *Killing Kennedy*, which broke ratings records and earned me a Screen Actors Guild best actor nomination, and along with my work that year on *Parks and Rec*, I am happily able to say that I am an actor working at both edges of my range, in comedy and drama, as a leading man and as a character actor. To do that is every actor's dream. Or should be.

My father-in-law, Norm, and I were very close. I was fond of him for so many reasons, not the least of which being that he said okay when I asked if I could marry his daughter. With the reputation I had at the time, and his penchant for gambling, I'm sure he was betting the over-under. But as Sheryl and I grew stronger and the years went by, he became an important part of our married life. He was like a character from *Guys and Dolls*, a lovable semi-wiseguy, part hustler and all heart. He had a unique and an adventurous past and had fantastic stories to show for it. He loved his daughter and he loved the grandsons she gave him.

When he had a massive and sudden heart attack, he was only sixty years old. I was in line in Starbucks when I got the call from Sheryl, who was distraught. We had to try to get to the hospital right away; the prognosis was grave.

I rushed home and collected Sheryl, who, in shock, was picking out the right shoes to wear for the occasion. Looking at her, pale and shaking, standing in a pile of footwear, I thought, "I need to remember this." I pulled her out of her trance and into the car.

At the hospital, we rushed to the emergency room. A doctor who looked disturbingly young barred the door. "You can't go in. We are fighting to save him," he said, closing it in our faces.

I led Sheryl to a quiet corner where we could watch the ER door. Time expanded and contracted, as it seems to do when crisis surrounds you. Minutes felt like hours and yet everything happened at once. I held my wife's hand but I didn't dare meet her eyes.

Eventually the ER door opened. The young doctor began to walk toward us.

"I need to remember this," I thought. His face betrayed no hint of the outcome. There was no "tell," which Norm, the inveterate poker player, would have been looking for in this ultimate moment of truth.

"This is just like you see in the movies," I thought as he opened his mouth to speak, yet in fact, it was nothing like the movies.

"I'm sorry. We did all we could." His eyes were sympathetic yet businesslike. He was appropriate and decent, but there was nothing more to say and so he didn't.

I held Sheryl as her knees gave way. Norm was the moon to her, bigger than life and always somewhere on the horizon. She was a little girl who had just lost her daddy. I held her as she cried.

I hope I was a good enough husband to her on that terrible day. I'm sure I could have been better somehow, maybe stronger or perhaps comforting in ways I didn't think of then. We got through it as well as could be expected and now, years later, I realize why my inner voice had split me off from the unfolding reality and had urged me to remember the awful details.

It's because I'm an actor. And actors play real life. Actors play doctors who give bad news and actors play daughters who lose their fathers and we play shock and horror and dismay and we can't do any of it, not honestly, unless we have been paying close attention to those moments in our own lives.

It can make you feel like a cipher, standing outside observing, taking mental notes. Or worse, like some vacant pretender, feeling and participating in the moment only partway, while you file away the details into the ever-expanding emotional toolbox you must fill to successfully ply your trade.

It is the details of human experience that matter. And as always, what even the most talented screenwriter could write pales in comparison.

———

When Arnold Schwarzenegger defied the skeptics and odds by running for governor of California, I was among the first and, as it turned out, somewhat shockingly, few members of our industry to actually work for his election. Arnold and I crisscrossed the state campaigning, raising money and doing the day-to-day grunt work necessary to get to the finish. In the end it was his not-so-secret weapon, Maria Shriver, who closed the deal, convincing Californians to buy into a postpartisan candidacy.

It was a tough fight and certainly no "gimme." California is a blue state and Arnold was going up against an incumbent Democrat. Having worked exclusively for that party all my life previously, I was putting my money where my mouth was for the first time as a newly converted independent voter. My days of being a knee-jerk supporter of *any* party were over for good. I now choose my candidates on any number of criteria, but never by party affiliation. Like "recreational" drug use, the idea of slavish party loyalty seems like an outdated and unhealthy concept. Certainly no one could think that the word "partisan" is anything other than pejorative.

At any rate, as the campaign drew to a close it had captured the attention of the world. Part of it was California's standing as the world's eleventh-biggest economy, and part of it was the attention that always follows Arnold, one of the great characters of our time. On election night every news outlet in the world was waiting in the ballroom at the Century Plaza Hotel. As with Ronald Reagan over three decades earlier, everyone wanted to know: could an actor become governor of the most important state of the most important country in the world?

Sheryl and I worked our way through presidential-level security up to the floor that had been secured for the campaign brain trust and members of the sprawling Shriver/Kennedy/Schwarzenegger clan. The hallway was thick with staffers, volunteers and huge men with Secret Service–style earpieces.

The drone of CNN and Fox News spilled from every room we passed as we made our way to the hotel's presidential suite.

I knocked on the door, but there was no answer. After a moment I saw that it was unlocked, so I opened it for Sheryl and I followed her in.

It was a huge suite, with a living room and hallways leading to additional seating areas and bedrooms. Few lights were on, so the giant glass windows glowed with a breathtaking panorama of the Los Angeles skyline. Unlike the crackling energy of the hallway outside, the room was as quiet as a tomb. A huge flat-screen TV was dormant, probably the only one in the hotel and probably one of the few in the country not in use at that moment, as the votes were almost in.

Sheryl and I looked at each other, wondering if maybe somehow we were in the wrong place. Then I saw a woman whom I hadn't noticed, sitting alone in the shadows. Although she was frail and old, her posture was ramrod straight. She had likewise not noticed our entrance. I moved closer and recognized her steel-blue eyes, which were gazing into the cityscape outside the suite's windows. Her eyes were afire, blazing with a passion and a sort of emotion I couldn't name. It was Eunice Kennedy Shriver.

I wondered if we should leave and not interrupt her private moment.

"Where is everyone?!?" she asked with authority, turning her gaze finally to Sheryl and me.

"I don't know, Mrs. Shriver," I replied. "I hope we aren't disturbing you."

"Not at all!" she said, crossing to the giant TV. "We should turn this on," she said, trying to navigate the remote.

I thought of all the elections she had watched before, for her brothers, for her husband. I was overcome with emotion to be so close to her, she who had been so close to history, she who had played such a role in creating it for so long.

Although I had spent time with her over the years at various family functions, it wasn't until very recently that we had gotten to know each other. Every year Maria and her brother Anthony hold a bike race as their fund-raiser for their Best Buddies charity for individuals with intellectual disabilities. One of the highlights being an extremely competitive bicycle-built-for-two race along a tight and dangerous course where a number of teams have gone ass-over-teakettle. At the last race Eunice had insisted I be her partner. I was shocked. I wasn't about to put her, at eighty-three years old, in a crash helmet on the back of a race bike.

"Come on, let's go!" she said, grabbing me by the shirt.

Desperately I looked to Maria for help. She gave me a look that could not have been more clear: "You see what I deal with?!" along with underpinnings of a huge and prideful love.

Mrs. Shriver and I finished second that day.

Back in the presidential suite, I knew to hop to it when Mrs. Shriver wanted something.

"Can you help me with this remote?" she asked.

At that moment the door burst open to a raucous crowd of supporters and family members led by the great Sargent Shriver, brandishing his cane like a drum major.

"Woo-hoo!" he yelled, as Maria, beautifully dressed for the occasion in a white and black Armani dress, helped him to a chair.

The technology gods, who so often forsake me, smiled this night, and I managed to click the remote to CNN.

Now the room was filling in earnest with the big donors, the campaign brain trust and every member of the family. Other than *Ghostbusters* director Ivan Reitman, there were few members of the entertainment community. The vibe was quiet, filled with tension, but with an unmistakable sense of occasion. I found Arnold's campaign manager, Steve Schmidt (later to be played by Woody Harrelson in HBO's Sarah Palin movie, *Game Change*).

"How's it looking?" I asked.

"Good," he answered tightly. I awaited some evidence to support the assessment but got none. Maria sat with her kids and her cousin Caroline Kennedy on the big couch staring intently at the TV. I looked at my watch—it was seven P.M. and the polls had just closed.

The CNN breaking-news theme played.

"We can now project that Arnold Schwarzenegger will become the thirty-eighth governor of the state of California."

Now, in a movie, the script would have had the room erupt, like New Year's Eve, with lots of shouting, hugging and victory fists in the air. But in *real life*, it turns out, the celebration, if you could even call it that, was subdued, dignified, quiet and imbued with a dreamlike quality that made you begin to doubt that it was really actually happening. There was happiness and there was giddiness, sure, but it was way, way down deep, covered over by the dawning realization of the scope of what had transpired and the almost incomprehensible level of responsibility now at hand. As my mother used to say, "Be careful what you wish for."

There was still no sign of the man of the hour, and now people really began to notice that Arnold had been AWOL, undoubtedly in a back room working on both a victory and, if needed, a concession speech.

"Can you fucking believe this?" said Ivan Reitman. "From *Kindergarten Cop* to governor."

And now everyone was talking excitedly, in a low buzz, the room animated by a collective desire to put the moment in context. It became hard to hear.

But it was quickly, deathly quiet again as someone holding a phone said, "It's Governor Davis calling." CNN can declare winners all they want, but as anyone who watched Bush–Gore remembers, it ain't over until someone cries uncle.

At the end of the big room's hallway, a door opened. It was Arnold, suddenly and improbably looking like a governor. I studied his face—again, the truth vampire in me wanting to file this away for the moment when I might need to play a victorious candidate, as I indeed would in *Brothers & Sisters* and *Killing Kennedy*. If I'd have played the candidate as beaming, acknowledging all my supporters with a smile, wink or handshake, luxuriating in an energetic and triumphant trot to the vanquished waiting on the phone, I would have gotten it completely wrong. The governor-elect's walk was purposeful yet slow. He met no one's eye; he stared straight ahead. There would be a time to hug his family and acknowledge friends, but that would be later.

This scene was not playing out as I had expected and I was trying to understand what I was seeing. People stood on either side as Arnold walked to the waiting phone. The wait felt excruciating, at least to me, but Arnold was in no hurry. He almost seemed unsure, a quality I *never* associate with him.

An aide handed him the phone. For a brief moment Arnold held it at his chest, almost on his heart, but I knew it was subconscious. I knew what I was looking at; I finally got what was happening here. I was watching someone step into their future, a man aware enough to understand that his life would never be the same and changes he would never see coming were part of success's bargain.

"Governor Davis, how are you?" Arnold said.

It'd been a fairly tough campaign and not without its personal vitriol in the final days, as is common, so I could only imagine that Governor Davis, if he were to be truthful, would have answered, "Not so good!"

I tried to get a clue from Arnold's face or body language as to what was being said on the other end of the line, but there was no indication. But clearly Governor Davis was doing all the talking.

Then after a moment, from Arnold, "Thank you."

Another shorter bit of listening, then, "Thank you . . . thank you so much. Bye."

Arnold hung up the phone. For the first time he looked around the room. "Governor Davis wanted to offer his congratulations on the victory and was very gracious."

In a TV show or movie, theme music would have played now,

and finally the winner would have smiled and people would certainly have rushed to him for the beginning of a huge celebration. But I noted that on this night, in real life, the crowd didn't know how to react. It waited to take its cue from how the winner would react, and he, unlike an actor playing a made-up governor-elect, had to focus on the next piece of business at hand. The victory speech was now moments away and would be seen all around the world. So Arnold and his staff headed back down the hallway to prepare. Nothing tangible, in fact, had really happened.

It's this kind of life detail that you can't write or act with total authenticity unless you've experienced it. You literally can't make it up. And if you try to, it will look, feel and play like you did.

Whether it's a death of a loved one or a life-changing event with the world watching, these are the kinds of big moments that are often the turning points in stories and performances. With a knowledge of life's details, the performance becomes the next challenge. And to do that, you have to build your "character."

I never had an acting teacher, unless you count my drama classes in junior high. I was fortunate to work at a high level from the time I was fifteen, so I didn't have time or need for the kind of traditional acting classes that most actors attend at some point. I learned by doing the actual deed, which I believe is the ideal.

(Sidebar: Remember how I discussed how much I will miss not having my son Matthew around when he leaves home? He has just cranked up his ever-present techno Studio 54–meets–Eastern European–authoritarian–marching–song music, making it next to impossible to write this. Can he go to college today?)

In 1993 I found out that one of my early favorite books, Stephen King's *The Stand*, was finally coming to the screen as an eight-hour miniseries for ABC.

I took a meeting with the executives at ABC and they offered me one of the great roles, Larry. The romantic wannabe rock singer and major hero.

I had other ideas.

"I want to play Nick Andros."

"The deaf-mute?" asked the exec.

"Yes."

"But he has no lines!" said the exec.

"Sure, I know, but I feel like it would be more of a challenge and for sure less expected than playing a sort of traditional romantic lead."

"You know he gets killed before the end? It's a smaller part than Larry."

"I'm okay with that," I said.

The group shared a look that said, "Hey, if that's what you want, what do we care?"

Later that week I got an offer to play the part.

And it is a great one. Nick is a bullied underdog, a lonely, sweet-natured survivor of the plague that has destroyed most of the world's population. And indeed, his lack of dialogue would force me to find new ways to communicate on-screen and bring focus to him in a cast of other standout parts.

One morning as I sat with my coffee, going over the voluminous screenplay written by Stephen King himself, Sheryl offered some advice.

"Why don't you get an acting coach?" she asked with the perfect amount of seriousness and guilelessness. Coming from anyone other than the one person in my life who I know without question has my best interests at heart, I might have taken offense, thinking, "After everything I've done, after all this time and success, you think I need an *acting coach*?!" But instead I stopped to consider what I had never considered.

"Like who?" I asked.

"Well, how about the one Michelle Pfeiffer, Geena Davis and that new kid Brad Pitt use?"

"Roy London?" I asked, referring to the current state-of-the-art acting Svengali.

"Yeah, that's the one."

I didn't overthink it. After all, what could be the worst that happened? I got nothing out of it and prepared the same way I had for years? I called Roy the next day and booked a meeting.

I saw him at his Hollywood apartment, in one of the great old buildings that stand as a reminder of a time when there was true glamour in that part of town. I was nervous. I had no idea what would unfold, how Roy liked to work or what the day's process would be. We sat at the kitchen table.

"I've read the entire miniseries, but I'd like you to tell me how you see yourself in this part," he said in an extremely casual way. As we sipped our coffees, there was no pressure or any sense that this was a "lesson" or "session" of any sort.

"Well obviously the challenge is playing a deaf-mute" (today I believe the proper term is "hearing and vocally impaired").

"Yes," said Roy, absently looking out the kitchen window.

"Clearly, I have no experience in this area, nothing to draw on, so I will probably do a lot of research. I need to know what it is like to not be able to communicate, to live without hearing."

"I see," said Roy.

"I've gotten the contacts to a number of schools for the deaf, I should spend time there, really immerse myself," I added.

Roy nodded.

"But here's my big idea. I have been deaf in my right ear since I got the mumps as a newborn. I've talked to some folks at UCLA and they can design a hearing-aid-like device that will put white noise into my good ear. I won't be able to hear at all! I could live like that for a few weeks and maybe even throughout the shoot."

"Or you could just consider the times in your own life when you are unable to hear," he said simply.

"What do you mean by that?" I asked.

He sighed deeply.

"Look, if you want to wear a blindfold and stumble around your house bumping into things to learn how to play 'blind,' you can do that. A lot of actors do. You can block your hearing and not speak. But great performances are based on truth. And the *truth* is that you, Rob Lowe, can hear and you can speak. To play otherwise is only adding a layer of falsehood to your performance. What you *must* do, in my opinion, is play this character as someone who hears and speaks, as *you* do, but chooses not to."

I was completely taken aback. "Wait a minute. You don't think I should play this character who *is* a deaf-mute as a deaf-mute?!"

"Exactly. Because the actor playing the part is not a deaf-mute."

"But that's the way it's written!"

"Who cares! The writer isn't playing the part. *You* are. And you hear and you speak and you need to be truthful. Actors should never play 'ideas,' 'concepts,' or even 'characters,' they play the truth and that's it. Believe me, that alone will be hard enough as it is."

Like most people in Hollywood I had believed that the tradition of immersing yourself in a foreign world was the highest form of character preparation possible. To do so was the hallmark of being a "Method" actor. Even the most inane gossip-TV tabloid entertainment reporter or actor-hating entertainment executive cowers in awe of the "Method actor." The "Method" is the last bastion of fear and respect for the craft. But like anything, it has been misused, trotted out in self-congratulatory movie-star magazine profiles for attention and, I suspect, led to a uniform style of performance that in the wrong hands can come across as extremely mannered and absolutely humorless.

Clearly, Roy London agreed. "Have you seen *Reservoir Dogs*?"

Of course I had; it had been Quentin Tarantino's debut sensation a year back.

"Well, one of my students played the guy who was tortured to death and spends three-quarters of the movie dead and tied to a chair."

"Sure, I know the part."

"Well, I told him since he has no experience being dead, and is in fact a healthy, live, wonderful actor, that he must never 'play dead.' He can truthfully be someone tied to a chair trying to *look* dead. Believe me, the difference is huge, and he got reviews actually mentioning his 'presence' on-screen, even as a dead body!"

"What did Quentin Tarantino think of his choice to not be dead?"

"Oh you must *never* tell anyone. Particularly the director!"

I am of the school that believes (oftentimes in spite of overwhelming evidence to the contrary) that the director is the most important person in filmmaking. My first boss was Francis Ford Coppola, after all. The idea of keeping a director in the dark on how you're going to tackle a role was unthinkable. But I was so blown away by this revolutionary and subversive idea that I began to warm to it. Roy and I planned to meet twice a week to dig deeper into the script.

Eventually, I found myself on location in Salt Lake City, playing a scene with Gary Sinise. I had determined that my character could speak and hear everything but led people to believe otherwise as a survival mechanism in the postapocalyptic world he was struggling with. Watching from the monitor, neither the director nor Stephen King had any idea their beloved Nick Andros, in my hands, could hear and speak. And I never told.

When *The Stand* aired, it broke ratings records, becoming one of the most-watched miniseries of all time. And Roy London was right.

Using our little secret, I received some of the best reviews of my career. And most importantly, I learned yet another technique to stow in my professional tool bag.

And all actors have their tricks. Since the Greeks grabbed the masks of comedy and tragedy, any thespian worth a lick has been figuring out ways to shine, to stand out and sometimes sandbag fellow performers. Our little weapons can be used for good or ill, to make a character more authentic or to throw someone else's under the bus.

It was always a surprise and a source of some consternation among both fans and the folks responsible for making The West Wing that Martin Sheen never won an Emmy for playing one of the landmark roles in TV history. Martin even began to refer to our annual pilgrimage to the awards as his "Passover." But everyone realized that Jed Bartlet had the bad luck to inhabit the same airwaves as another titan of characterization, the late James Gandolfini, who was playing Tony Soprano. And pound for pound (no pun intended), there was no comparison.

With no disrespect to Martin, if you try hard enough, you can almost imagine a West Wing without President Bartlet (in fact, toward the end there was one, with Jimmy Smits center stage), but The Sopranos without Tony is a nonstarter. James Gandolfini's performance made that show, just as Aaron Sorkin's writing made The West Wing. After all, who wouldn't love a Nobel Prize–winning, multiple sclerosis–conquering, Latin-speaking, chain-smoking president of the United States, who also happened to love his staff like his own family? But to make a mob boss who interrupts his daughter's college tour to strangle a man to death with his bare hands empathetic, that requires some heavy lifting. Gandolfini won a boatload of awards and got the reviews of a lifetime (as well as the paychecks) because he humanized a monster. He made us love Tony Soprano in spite of Tony Soprano.

And he did it in a number of ways, from tapping into a reservoir of complex inner pain, sadness and kindness, to being sneaky funny with his hilarious malapropisms. But I think the key to humanizing Tony Soprano was his use of one of the great and surprisingly difficult actor tricks of all time, which is also the simplest: eating food on camera.

Tony stuffed his face at every opportunity. Cannoli, calzones, ice cream—there wasn't an episode where he didn't eat and eat a lot. And here's the secret: when actors eat, it subtly says to the audience, I have hunger, like you, so I am eating, like you. Like you, I am a real human being. It's very simple and it works every time.

There is one catch. It's an absolute nightmare to do. Next time you watch a movie or a TV show and it's one of those endless dinner scenes (*Brothers & Sisters*, anyone?), notice that almost never do you actually see food entering anyone's mouths. There's a lot of knife and fork holding and what I call "napkin acting," but almost no one ever eats. If you are lucky you might see someone on-screen take a drink.

On a certain level you don't connect with the noneating actors because you can't relate to a dinner where no one eats! And let's be plain: performances are made and broken in the audience's unconscious. So when Jimmy Gandolfini wolfs down a sub while planning a hit, you believe someone's gonna get whacked.

But this is a hard trick to pull off. Very few of us could be one of those professional eaters. I know I couldn't. I wish I could be more like Brad Pitt, who munches his way through many of his movies and has an Oscar nomination for *Moneyball* to show for it. But I'm a pussy when it comes to eating. An average scene takes anywhere from three to six hours to shoot. (I once shot one scene for *Forrest Gump's* director, Bob Zemeckis, for three *days*. On-screen it played for maybe ninety seconds.) Over that time, multiple angles of the same activity are shot, so if you take one sip of water and you want it to be on camera, you will have to take that sip every single time you do the scene.

Very few can eat or drink for hours on end. I still laugh out loud when I watch one of my early movies, *Class*. There is one of those dinner scenes, and Jacqueline Bisset puts a bit of salad in her mouth that is literally the size of a newborn baby's pinkie nail.

But there was also Danny Glover, whom I had the pleasure of working with on *Brothers & Sisters*. Sitting at one of those torturous and never-ending Walker family dinners, one of my favorite actors divided his time between cell phone calls to third-world leaders and gobbling every single piece of food that wasn't nailed to the floor. At one point, after eating his entire "fake meal" for the umpteenth time, he leaned over to his assistant.

"I heard there are going to be some chili dogs at catering. Can you let me know when they're ready?"

I couldn't believe it; this guy was in terrific shape. He must have a hollow leg. He took on-set eating to Oscar-caliber levels.

———————

There are many hallmarks of bad acting, but one of the most common is when actors stare unblinkingly into each other's eyes, rooted to the spot where they stand as they play their scene. Turn on a daytime soap and you will see this style. In real life, we rarely "eye-screw" each other while we talk, unless we are arguing heavily or flirting passionately. Instead we live our lives while we talk, we move, we turn away, we read the paper, unpack groceries or check our phones. Nine times out of ten, in real life, what you are doing is much more important than what you are saying.

For some reason, some actors (and a lot of bad writers and directors) believe otherwise. The writers think their "words" are the most important part of any scene and the actors want to make sure nothing interferes with how clearly they can be seen on camera, preferably in close-up. So you see actors standing around, "acting."

But look at your favorite movie moments and I bet you see scenes played while folding laundry, making breakfast, doing office work or "walking and talking" down hallways. Life has tasks. If you perform them on-screen, you look *real*.

Working with everyday objects is called "prop work" in acting parlance and most of us are good at it. It can be harder than you think; the cast of *ER* was among the best ever, with IV bags being hung, rubber gloves snapped on, electrodes placed, all while they delivered some pretty complex dialogue. No standing around for them.

On *The West Wing*, Richard Schiff, one of the best scene stealers of all time, would routinely enter what was ostensibly someone else's scene, carrying seventeen files, a briefcase, a thermos and a half-eaten sandwich. I don't think he ever entered on a unicycle spinning plates, but he may have.

And the result? You can't take your eyes off him. If he dropped a file and picked it up, you could have been delivering the Gettysburg Address and no one would have been looking at you. The masters of "prop acting" can kill you with one flip of a spatula or one perfectly placed puff of a cigarette.

Don't kid yourself. Acting is both a symbiotic team sport and also a kill-or-be-killed individual death match. To the victor goes the bigger trailer.

I once had to face down the legendary Dame Maggie Smith. She is world-renowned for stealing every scene she is in, sometimes with no lines needed. Just an arched eyebrow and grown movie stars lie in piles like the aftermath of the Battle of Bull Run. (Watch her in *Downton Abbey* to see what I mean. She's genius.) I was determined that I wouldn't get mauled by the great Dame. So I plotted.

The amazing Richard Eyre was directing us in a filmed version of Tennessee Williams's classic *Suddenly, Last Summer*. Maggie had the throw-down role of Violet Venable. I had the incredibly one-note part of Dr. Cukrowicz. (Played by Montgomery Clift in the movie version.) My part consisted mainly of investigating her role in the death of her son.

"How did it happen?" I would ask. She would then have a four-paragraph aria.

"Tell me more," I would reply, and another brilliant monologue would follow. And so on.

But at one point, she asked my character to hand her a lighter for her cigarette. I used this tiny part in the script to have my little bit of fun.

I asked the prop master to supply me with a book of matches that was empty, save the last two. About a page before she was required to ask for a lighter for herself, I chose to pull out a smoke, light one match to no avail and then light the last one. Unable to light my smoke, I let it dangle in my lips sadly until the next page, where she asked for the lighter.

Now I had created a new moment out of this bit of prop work where she watched me struggle with my matches without offering her lighter until she wanted it herself. It gave my character a little added conflict with hers, where before there was none. In a scene that was all about her, I created a tiny moment for me.

When people talk about the "craft" of acting, it's these sorts of techniques they mean. Like any other artisan, actors who have the tools use them to accomplish what they are paid to do: build interesting, entertaining, honest, believable characters who tell the story in the appropriate fashion.

I once made a very successful love story with an actress who went on to become a great star. Like any potential star, she knew her way around her craft as well as her strengths and weaknesses. At the climax of the movie, she had a very long and emotionally demanding scene where she confronted me about our relationship's future. The screenplay had her start vulnerable, become angry and finally be almost incapacitated by tears. Knowing that we weren't making a play, that movies and TV are beholden to the god of editing anyway, she never, not once, gave all three of those emotions in the same take.

She did a version vulnerable. She did a version angry, and finally, she did a version weeping from start to finish. She let the editors cut all three takes together, making her look like Meryl Streep. I've never seen anyone do that since, and you can't get away with that onstage, but in that instance it worked and worked brilliantly, so who the hell cares how it was accomplished?

Directors have their own tricks as well.

I had been romantically involved with an actress I was starring opposite, but it had ended well before we began shooting. In fact, she was already well into a painful on-again, off-again relationship. Our director knew this history.

We were deep into shooting a pivotal scene but hadn't captured any real pain; in spite of some very good writing, the scene had no explosiveness. The director, inexperienced but very smart, pulled me aside and said, "Wait until we do her close-up and then tell her you don't love her anymore." Just his saying this to *me* made me emotional. The breakup dialogue was nuanced and subtle. This ad lib would be a cruel hammer. My former lover and costar didn't know what I was wielding as the take began. I waited for the moment. "I don't love you anymore."

Her face quivered slightly. She tried to shake it off, but she was clearly stunned, like she'd been slapped but didn't want anyone to know it hurt. But the camera saw everything, as always. She was in a big "Warner Bros. haircut"–style close-up, so as she lost the battle for composure and dignity, the glacier cracked wide open and she sobbed.

The trick opened her up. It's the best scene in the movie.

Ad libs, in my experience, are either great, out-of-this-world additions or horrific, borderline-embarrassing utterances that send a scene to the bottom of the ocean. Some of the most renowned and talented actors I've worked with were terrible ad libbers. I'm not sure why this is, but when it comes to making verbal adjustments on the fly, many are called, few are chosen. You need to learn to be self-reliant. The script may be weak; a scene that seemed great on the page may suddenly not work on the set—you never know what obstacle will be thrown in front of your performance. I once starred in a big miniseries that culminated with the villain giving a two-page monologue trying to goad me into killing him. The actor playing the bad guy wanted to ad lib his own version of the movie-ending speech. Although he was playing a vampire, he went into a soliloquy about being a cowboy.

The director was not impressed.

After a very tense negotiation, the actor was forced to shit-can his self-penned opus and stick to the original script. There was only one problem: He hadn't bothered to learn it. Cue cards were made and placed next to my head while we filmed his part of the scene. When it was time to turn the camera onto me, he was sent home. My part of the scene called for me to listen to this very intricate two-page speech and run a wide range of emotions at very specific times. The director offered to have the script supervisor read the departed actor's lines.

I've long since learned that when faced with a problem, you should rip off the Band-Aid, acknowledge the problem and cut your losses.

"Just turn on the camera, I'll do it without anyone."

I did the two-minute pivotal close-up reacting to my own imagining of what the speech *should* have been like while staring at a strip of duct tape marking where the actor should have been.

Like life, moviemaking is never exactly what you think it will be. Sometimes it's great when you think it's gonna be a turkey, and sometimes even a ship of fools becomes *Battleship Potemkin*. You can go to all of the acting classes you want, you can be first in your class at the fanciest film schools, but you're never going to know what to expect until you *do* it. And then do it some more.

I have nothing against film or acting schools. Many huge talents have come out of both, and lots of folks who are more accomplished and better storytellers than I will ever be owe them a great debt.

But today, anyone can make a movie on their phone. You can edit a film on a midrange laptop at the same level as the pros. Today, no filmmaker has an excuse to not make his movie. As the man says: "Just do it."

And as for acting classes, drama schools, et al., let me say this: I'm thinking about opening one of my own. It won't be a four-year impossible-to-get-into school; I'll take anyone. It won't be expensive, and as long as your check clears, you are in. You can enroll and graduate in a day. I'm calling it Film Acting School. In just one day, students will experience the *reality* of filmmaking.

Here is the breakdown of the course:

4:00 A.M.: You will be required to report to a location via directions that you will receive in the middle of the night, slipped under your door. They will be incorrect.

4:05 A.M.: You will be ushered into a makeup trailer, where you will begin having a prosthetic face applied. (There will be a variety to choose from, fat man or woman, old-age face and creature from *Star Trek: Voyager.*)

5:00 A.M.: Halfway through the makeup process, you will be provided your speech,* to be filmed with a full professional crew as a lifetime keepsake and the culmination of your course.

5:30 A.M.: The catering truck will arrive to provide you breakfast. At this point your prosthetic will be 80 percent complete, so you will have to eat through a straw.

6:00 A.M.: Face completed.

6:30 A.M.: You will be provided with your accommodations for the shoot, an eight-and-a-half-by-four-foot room with an open toilet called a honey wagon. For an added fee of just seventeen cents, FAS Studios will provide a working heater and/or air conditioner.

6:45 A.M.: The director will stop by for a meeting to discuss any ideas you may have about the upcoming scene.

6:46 A.M.: The meeting ends. The second assistant director will be introduced to you. He will provide all information related to the day's shooting schedule.

6:50 A.M.: Your wardrobe arrives. Although you will have provided your measurements in advance, nothing will fit.

7:05 A.M.: New wardrobe arrives. The costumer apologizes for its being 100 percent wool.

7:10 A.M.: The second AD brings you water and says, "Hydrate. It's going to

---

* You can choose whatever great speech you want memorialized and commit it to memory before-hand if you wish. The Film Acting School LLC does not guarantee any speech can be shot due to a number of possible unforeseen or force majeure situations that may arise, including, but not limited to, weather, illness, mechanical malfunctions, and personnel changes due to scheduling conflict, miscommunication, bad information, tardiness, nonperformance, incapacitation, drugs or death.

be one hundred ten degrees today." He also gives you a twenty-minute warning for your scene's rehearsal.

9:10 A.M.: The second AD returns and tells you they are "ready, ready" (for whatever reason, no one just says "ready" anymore in show business). You hop into a white van for the ride to set.

9:20 A.M.: The van departs.

9:25–10:00 A.M.: You rehearse your speech with a full crew.

10:05 A.M.: You are dropped back off at your honey wagon. The AD gives you an estimate of forty-five minutes for the crew to light the set and to begin shooting.

10:06–10:40 A.M.: Final moments to prepare for the scene.

10:55 A.M.: AD arrives and says they have decided to shoot another sequence first and will update you as information comes in.

12:45–1:00 P.M.: Lunch (through a straw).

1:05 P.M.: After-lunch "touch-ups" of your prosthetic head, in the makeup trailer.

2:00–3:30 P.M.: Free time in your trailer.

3:45 P.M.: AD tells you he will have more information on when you will shoot in forty-five minutes and will give you a fifteen-minute warning before they are ready.

3:46 P.M.: AD returns to say they are ready.

4:30 P.M.: After rehearsing on set and final makeup, hair and wardrobe checks, it's time to shoot your big speech; everyone gets into position.

4:31 P.M.: "Roll camera" is called.

4:31:30 P.M.: A dog begins barking in a house nearby, preventing any sound recording.

4:45 P.M.: A neighbor receives $500 to lock his dog in the garage.

5:00 P.M.: You finally shoot your first take. It will be unusable due to a focus problem with the camera.

5:05–5:30 P.M.: Multiple takes will be attempted. None will be completed. Among the problems will be other actors who don't know their lines, too much sweat pouring from your prosthetic face, a flare in the lens, a "hair in the gate," a helicopter circling, a jet landing, a boom microphone in the shot, bystanders wandering by in the background and a guy who wants $5,000 to turn off his leaf blower. The director takes you aside for a stern talking-to. "We are losing light. If you don't give us a usable take *now*, we will have to scrap the scene."

After being on set for thirteen hours, you will have approximately four minutes of ideal conditions to shoot your big scene.

Maybe you can pull it off, maybe you can't.

If this sounds like something that interests you, you may have what it takes to be a working actor in the film business. And it won't take you four years of drama school to find out.

With fellow Best Actor nominee James Gandolfini at the Emmys.

A Boy

I'm trying to remember when I felt like this before. Like an elephant is sitting on my chest, like my throat is so tight and constricted that I can feel its tendons, like my eyes are 100 percent water, spilling out at will, down pathways on my face that have been dry for as long as I can think of. I'm trying to remember: When was the last time my heart was breaking?

The death of my mother was one time, but her passing was prolonged enough to let me prepare for it, to the extent anyone can. At the most intense moment, sitting at her gravesite, I felt like I could hear every leaf blower in a fifty-mile radius, felt as if I could feel the sun's rays turning my skin darker shades with each second, my skin irritated and jumpy, making me want to crawl out of it. I'm feeling it all now again, but no one has died.

When I was a boy, I had to leave my friends in the summer, just as Malibu was becoming Malibu, say good-bye to my first girlfriend and go to Ohio to stay with my dad. There is a little of that sense memory at play too, a feeling that I'm about to be left out of important events, separated from life as I know it, the world as I love it.

I am remembering and feeling the details of my parents' divorce and our family's forced march out of my home to an alien world across the country. The good-byes to my father and my beloved grandparents; rationally I knew I would see them all again, but now I have the same body-deadening weight of the condemned, counting the minutes until the final moments of a life that's all I've ever known. This encompassing, exhausting sadness I had mostly forgotten, or buried, until now.

Today is my son Matthew's last night home before college.

I have been emotionally blindsided. I know that this is a rite many have been through, that this is nothing unique. I know that this is all *good* news; my son will go to a great school, something we as a family have worked hard at for many years. I know that this is his finest hour. But looking at his suitcases on his bed, his New England Patriots posters on the wall and his dog watching him pack, sends me out of the room to a hidden corner where I can't stop crying.

Through the grief I feel a rising embarrassment. "Jesus Christ, pull yourself together, man!" I tell myself. There are parents sending their kids off to battle zones, or putting them into rehabs and many other more legitimately emotional situations, all over our country. How dare I feel so shattered? What the hell is going on?

One of the great gifts of my life has been having my two boys and, through them, exploring the mysterious, complicated and charged relationship between fathers and sons. As I try to raise them, I discover the depth and currents of not only our relationship but ones already downstream, the love and loss that flowed between my father and me and how that bond is so powerful.

After my parents' divorce, when I was four, I spent weekends with my dad, before we finally moved to California. By the time Sunday rolled around, I was incapable of enjoying the day's activities, of being in the moment, because I was already dreading the inevitable good-bye of Sunday evening. Trips to the mall, miniature golf or movies had me in a foggy, lump-throated daze long before my dad would drop me home and drive away.

Now, standing among the accumulation of the life of a little boy he no longer is, I look at my own young doppelgänger and realize: it's me who has become a boy again. All my heavy-chested sadness, loss and longing to hold on to things as they used to be are back, sweeping over me as they did when I was a child.

In front of Matthew I'm doing some of the best acting of my career. I've said before that the common perception that all good actors should be good liars is exactly the opposite; only bad actors lie when they act. But now I'm using the tricks of every hack and presenting a dishonest front to my son and wife. To my surprise, it appears to be working. I smile like a jack-o'-lantern and affect a breezy, casual manner. Positive sentences only and nothing but enthusiasm framing my answers to Matthew's questions.

"Do you think it's cold in the dorms in the winter?" he asks in a voice that seems smaller than it was just days ago.

"Naah!" I lie, having no idea what his new room for the next four years will be like.

This line of questioning is irrelevant anyway, as Sheryl is preparing for any possible scenario, as is her genius. We all have our strengths; among hers is the ability to put anything a human being could possibly need in a suitcase. Or box. Or FedEx container. She is channeling her extraordinary love and loss into a beautiful display of preparing her son for his travels. And in the end, Arctic explorers will travel lighter.

Matthew's dog, Buster, watches me watching Matthew as he sorts through his winter jackets. I am one of those people who believe dogs can actually smile, and now I can expand that belief to include an ability to look incredulous as well. Buster seems to be the only member of our family to see what a wreck I am, and he is having none of it.

"You disgust me," he seems to say, looking at me with his chocolate eyes. "Get a backbone, man!"

The clothes are off the bed and zipped into the bags. The bed is tidy and spare; it already has the feel of a guest bed, which, I realize to my horror, it will become. I replay wrapping him in his favorite blanket like a burrito. This was our nightly ritual until the night he said in an offhanded way, "Daddy, I don't think I need blanky tonight." (And I thought that was a tough evening!)

I think of all the times we lay among the covers reading, first me to him, *Goodnight Moon* and *The Giving Tree*, and later him to me: my lines from *The West Wing* or a movie I was shooting. The countless hours of the History Channel and *Deadliest Catch*; the quiet sanctuary where I could sneak in and grab some shut-eye with him when I had an early call time on set, while the rest of the house was still bustling. I look at the bed and think of all the recent times when I was annoyed at how late he was sleeping. I'll never have to worry about that again, I realize. I make up an excuse to leave the room and head to my secret corner.

For his part, Matthew has been a rock. He is naturally very even-keeled, rarely emotional; he is a logical, tough pragmatist. He would have made a great Spartan. True to form, he is treating his impending departure as just another day at the office. And I'm glad. After all, *someone's* gotta be strong about this.

Our youngest, Johnowen, will be staying behind and returning to high school, and now it's time for them to say good-bye. I've been worried about how Johnowen will handle the departure of his big brother. Only two years apart, they share most of the same friends, which is to say that Johnny hangs with all the older boys who are also leaving home. My sons are very close in that vaguely annoyed constant companionship that brothers can share (if they are lucky). Now what will happen to their NFL rivalry and smack talk? The nightly ear-splitting deconstructing of Scandinavian dubstep EDM? The incessant wrangling about what guys and what girls are coming by and when? Life is breaking up the team that kept me in loving consternation until all hours of the morning and throughout those never-ending summer nights.

I am a boy again as I wonder: What will become of my two closest friends?

In the driveway Matthew gives Johnowen a laconic high five. "Peace," he says, clearly going out of his way to avoid any emotion or drama. Johnowen, whose passion runs just barely under the surface, is a little taken aback. He looks at me, sad and bemused, and I know what he is thinking: "That's my brother! A cool cucumber till the end." He watches Matthew hop into the car for the ride to the airport.

Of the many horrors of divorce, the most egregious is that it robs a kid of the best of both worlds. Dads can do many things that even the best moms can't, and vice versa. I've always been fascinated by whom my kids come to and for what purpose, whether they are drawn to Sheryl or to me, and I've noted that it always surprises me which one of us they need for comfort or advice and when.

On the plane, we have two seats together and one apart. Matthew chooses to sit with Sheryl and I see how happy it makes her. Then on go the headphones and not a word is shared for most of the flight. Sheryl and I look at each other and smile. "Teenagers."

An amber, evening light fills the cabin as we flee the setting sun, heading east. I've taken a break from reading and am staring at my boy. The light from his window is cutting across his face, accentuating his cheekbones and strong jawline, making him look unbearably handsome and grown-up. He might as well be a young businessman headed to a meeting.

His favorite headphones are on and he is reading, so I can consider him in freedom, without his awareness. I remember the first time I laid eyes on him in the delivery room. "He's blond!" was my first thought. And I remember what I whispered to him when his eyes opened for the first time in his life as he peered in my face, and (I am convinced) into my soul. "Hello, I'm your daddy. And I will always be there for you."

Sheryl has looked up from her iPad and mouths to me, "Are you okay?" I want to be, for her; I don't need her worrying about anything other than the logistics ahead, and I certainly don't want to draw any attention on the plane. But something about her face and the way she is looking at me, while I am looking at him, pulls the rug out again and I avert my eyes from her, from him; my sunglasses go on and I open up a newspaper, covering my entire face and anything that anyone might see, like a bad version of Maxwell Smart hiding from a KAOS agent. I am amazed that so much water can come out of the eyes of someone who dehydrates himself with so much caffeine.

Just as we land, I take one more peek at Matthew. If he has any emotion about any of this, he is not showing it. I'm proud that he is charging into this chapter that opens the narrative of his adult life with such confidence. And I sneak another peek at Sheryl and allow myself to think, "All of this is exactly as it needs to be."

———

It's move-in day. We drive onto the historic, grand and beautifully intimidating campus with our rental car packed with Matthew's belongings. Stuck in a nonmoving lineup of cars filled with other parents in the same emotional boat, I am cursed again with idle time to contemplate the day ahead of me. But today, for the first time, the overpowering melancholy is gone, the bittersweet nostalgia too, replaced by an envious, excited adrenaline. To be at the true beginning! To be moments away from meeting strangers, some of whom will be in, and change, the course of your life forever! To have the opportunity an elite university provides to be able to discover yourself, your true *adult self*, away from any of the tentacles of childhood! I feel the gooseflesh rising from my arms.

I didn't go to college. At seventeen, I left home to go on location for my first movie. The first private space of my own wasn't a dorm room; it was a hotel room in Tulsa, Oklahoma. I didn't have to navigate a brand-new, totally foreign ecosystem of fellow students and faculty; I was thrown unceremoniously into a strange group of actors and crew members. And I had the knowledge that for good or bad, it would all be over in three months, not four years. Now, for the first time that I can think of, I have no personal life experience to draw from to guide my son. My first and only college experience will be through him.

Unloading in front of the Gothic-style dorm, the welcoming upperclassmen do crazy, exuberant dances and grab boxes to help. These are the RAs of the dorm, the first bit of much new collegiate vocabulary I will learn along with my son.

He and I leave Sheryl to do her masterwork in his corner, hardwood-floored room. She will handle the important groundwork of his comfort for the next year. I will handle other issues: finding the best pizza, finding a gym where he can continue jujitsu, the purchase of a bicycle and where to stash it. Sheryl's immaculate and detailed renovation is an OCD and maternal-love-fueled epic poem of logistics and labor, so Matthew and I have plenty of time to explore and just spend time together.

I'm surprised at how little we say to each other, and how good that feels. There is nothing we are withholding and I know that our "being current" with each other, as the shrinks would say, is a result of years spent in each other's company. Not just dinner or good-nights or drop-offs; it's time coaching his teams, being in the stands, on fishing boats, in the water surfing or diving, watching stupid television, being home on nights when he is with his friends and talking smack with them, standing up to and getting in the face of teachers, parents, other kids or anyone who so much as thought about treating him badly.

We put in the time together; we built this thing we have of comfort and love. And now, as we both prepare to let go of each other, it is paying off. That evening, even though his dorm room is ready he says, "Dad, I think I'll just stay with you and Mom tonight." I catch Sheryl's eye; this time, it's hers that are moist.

The next morning, after all of the freshmen file out of the massive and imposing chapel after convocation, Matthew shows his first signs of uncertainty. The president's speech was an ode to the incoming achievers, "the most highly accomplished" class ever accepted in "the most competitive year" in the school's history. It took this elegant ceremony, in a setting both beautiful and intimidating, among a sea of strangers, some of the best kids our country has to offer, for Matthew to realize the stakes. He did it. This is real. He is here. This is happening.

"Dad, what if it's too hard for me here?" he asks me later, sitting on his fold-out bed back at the hotel, looking more "fresh" than "man."

"You came from a *very* tough academic school with great grades. You took the tests, you got the scores, you did the hours and you did the travel and extracurriculars. You made it happen. No one else. This won't be any different. This school chose you because *they know* you can succeed here."

"None of the other kids look scared at all," he says, and for the first time I can remember since he was a baby, I can see his eyes welling up. I want to reach out and hug him, but I don't. Instead I look him in the eye.

"*Never* compare your insides to someone else's outsides."

He nods and turns away.

"I think I might take a nap."

"Sure, I'll wake you in a while," I say.

He curls up in a ball, like he used to. I unfold a blanket and cover him, tucking it underneath, rolling him in it, like a burrito.

The students who populate the university are impressive. These are the ones who didn't dumb it down to be cool, the ones who were unabashed about learning and loved doing it. Anyone feeling anxious about the future of our country should spend a couple of days on our college campuses. These kids are studs.

Matthew meets friends quickly, a great group of freshmen from all over the country.

"Dad, they all can't believe I left Southern California. They all want to go there."

"This is exactly how you will get to live in Southern California if you want to. You will earn it *here*," I tell him at a good-bye dinner Sheryl and I have put together for him and his new pals. He nods in his solemn way.

After dinner the gang plans on going to one of the local nightspots. "Dad, you gotta come!" He insists, and I know, like me, he is playing to delay the end of the evening. I leave before sunrise in the morning.

Sheryl will stay later (I have to be back at *Parks and Recreation* by noon to shoot a full day) and she urges me to go. "Do it. He wants to be with you. I'll drop you off."

But at the hot spot it is wall-to-wall kids, easily a couple hundred of them, raucous and spilling out into the street. I know I can't wade into a group like that unnoticed. Matthew knows it too.

"Honey, I can't go in there," I say as everyone piles out of our rental car.

"I know, Dad."

We lock eyes for the tiniest beat. I want to see what, if anything, he will say. His new "bros" are already striding to the club and he doesn't want to be left behind. This is the college good-bye I've heard so much about and dreaded so deeply.

I close in to hug him, but he puts just one arm around me, a half hug.

"Peace," he says, a phrase I'd never heard him use until he said the same thing to his little brother in the driveway.

Then he turns on his heel and strides away. From his body language I know he won't turn to look back; I know why and I'm glad.

I watch him until I can't see him anymore, until he's swallowed up by his new friends and his new life.

Our house is not the same now. Sheryl and Johnowen and I, overnight, have a completely different dynamic. Quieter, gentler, deeper in some ways that I cannot understand. Matthew's dog, Buster, has stopped eating, which is maybe not a bad thing considering his weight issues. I had a five thirty A.M. call on set the next day and I used it as an excuse to sleep in Matthew's room. I told myself I did it to have some quiet to get to bed early.

My children have always made me *feel*. They have always taught me, changed me, always for the better. I hope I have been the best dad I could be and that I have succeeded more than I failed. Having them in my life turned me into a man. Now, with my long-distance longing and worry, covered by electric excitement about the future for Matthew, I realize that saying good-bye to him has turned me into a boy.

And now, we will both grow up.

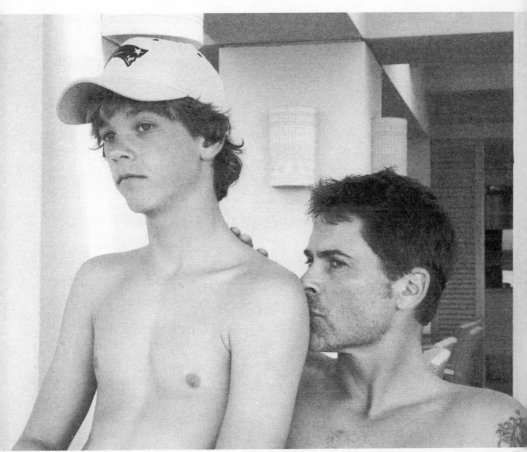
With my favorite Patriots fan.

The 99 Percent

I love acting. I love what I get to do for a living. It's one of the greatest blessings of my life. I never lose sight of the fact that so many work at jobs that are merely that—jobs—that so many put in their efforts mainly so they can go home and do what they *really* want to do. It's much easier for me to get up at four thirty A.M. to go to a job I'm passionate about than it is for some to go to a job they are indifferent to.

However, as the British would say, I very much enjoy "taking the piss" out of my line of work. It's not that I don't value my industry, it's that oftentimes we have it coming. I'm sure there are more than a few examples of tomfoolery in show business in these pages but it's because I have such an affection for my fellows and the knowledge that sometimes we all could be better, both as performers and people. I'm never more aware of this than when I see one of my own performances or replay an interaction with my friends, family or coworkers and think, "I can be better than this."

I want to live up to my heroes. It's well-known that there's always someone better than you are: more talented, more famous, richer, smarter, better looking. Someone is always doing something better than you are and being better rewarded for it. There isn't a person on earth who isn't part of this 99 percent in some fashion. But I never feel envy; I'm not resentful or jealous. I don't begrudge the elite. I worship at the altar of the elite. These are not folks to vilify or use as political fodder. For me, these are the North Stars to be used as guides to the places I still hope to go. They are my inspiration.

It would be great to live in a culture where a genius like George Lucas doesn't have to inoculate himself against criticism of his making a huge profit selling *Star Wars* to Disney by announcing he is "giving most of it away" to charity. It's not our business what he does with the rewards of his genius, whether it's four dollars or four billion dollars. What matters is: He came from nowhere, no one handed him anything and by the power of his mind he built an empire that brought joy to millions. He has earned the right to answer to no one.

I am an unabashed fan of earned, deserved success.

Sure, when I read *Jerry Maguire* I thought, "I would kill in that role!" But to see my old pal Tom Cruise in the scene where he goes from being "the master of the living room" to the naked vulnerability of "you complete me" makes me want to weep, not out of envy, but because *he is a man fulfilling his potential.* When someone is blessed with "their moment" and crushes it, it's deeply moving for me. Seeing Catherine Zeta-Jones in *Chicago* revealing herself as a world-class song-and-dance woman or discovering a new face like Christophe Waltz asking, "Are you harboring enemies of the state?" in *Inglourious Basterds* turns me back into that little boy who fell in love with the movies. And in today's jaded, bottom-line-minded world, I'm grateful for it.

One of my wife Sheryl's big movies as a makeup artist was *Glengarry Glen Ross*, starring her client Al Pacino. I came east to visit her and sat one day in the shadows to watch. All the lions of the screen were there: Al, Jack Lemmon, Ed Harris, Kevin Spacey and Alan Arkin. But the scene to be filmed that day was one where their characters were all to be schooled by a young interloper from the head office, to be played by my friend Alec Baldwin. Now, Alec can carry his own water, and he had plenty of experience and success coming into this day, but I don't care who you are, if you are doing a three-page monologue where it is incumbent on you to outshine a murderers' row like that group, there are no guarantees.

I chatted with Sheryl, had espresso with Al and then pulled up to an apple box in the shadows to watch Alec shoot the big scene.

What I witnessed was one of the largest beat-downs an actor has ever delivered. Alec's "always be closing" sequence in *Glengarry Glen Ross* would become iconic. The writing was breathtaking and the right actor was there at the right time; he had only to execute, and he did. I had hairs standing up on the back of my neck.

Al and the greats seemed appropriately stunned, although no one overtly noted the ass-kicking Alec had just delivered. (Although I thought I noticed one of them doing a less-than-perfect job of covering his professional jealousy. And it shows in that actor's performance in the scene.)

The writing and the acting on that day continue to inspire me. My line of work, like most jobs I'm sure, can sometimes be demoralizing, maybe even a little boring. But whenever I'm feeling "over it," that maybe I've been at this for too long and it's all a little bloodless, I know what to do. I go to YouTube and type in "Alec Baldwin, always be closing speech." And I'm fifteen again, in love with movies, with acting and feeling the full throttle of my abilities and passion to use them. I'm ready to walk through walls again.

When I was approached by Ridley Scott's company to play JFK in *Killing Kennedy*, one of the reasons I said yes was my hunch that playing one of my heroes would be a deep source of inspiration. And I was right. All of the weeks spent dissecting his famous voice, the endless hours watching obscure archival footage, hoping to find a clue to his character, a toehold to climb over the barrier of his almost impenetrable iconography and find the mortal man inside, was sheer bliss. It was humbling and exhilarating to be given the opportunity to bring him back to life for a brief, shining moment. And I didn't want to screw it up.

There is nowhere to hide when you are playing Kennedy in a movie called *Killing Kennedy* based on the bestseller of the same name that will be plastered on every billboard, nine stories high in Times Square, marketed throughout the world and shown in one hundred seventy countries. If you are bad in the role, a lot of folks will know about it. I guess I'm practical enough to be aware of that but experienced enough to forget about it. Big stakes don't mean you develop or play a role any differently. It's impossible to play "a martyred hero." But it *is* possible to play a man.

I looked for the human details. I found he wore reading glasses but hated being photographed in them. He nervously took them in and out of his breast pocket, which is why you often could barely see his scrunched-down pocket square. I wore his cologne (Jockey Club) and I figured out his very particular body language and distinctive walk. I learned to flout the fashion police by buttoning *both* buttons on my two-button suits, like he always did. Like a vampire, I sucked every ounce of obscure (obvious traits aren't really useful) info out of the public record and into the building of my interpretation of the man I have admired for so long.

That the performance was well received and that *Killing Kennedy* was a ratings success is obviously gratifying. Ironically, it also earned me a Best Actor nomination from my peers in the Screen Actors Guild alongside Sheryl's old client, Al Pacino. But what I think about going forward isn't the results, however positive. What inspires me is that I can still be moved by the mysterious and ultimately unknowable process of discovering a character. In my fourth decade of doing this, I can, sometimes, if the circumstances are right, get that giddy, awestruck, trembly feeling as an actor when the lightbulb goes on and I have an "Aha!" moment. It keeps me wanting to stay at it.

When you can no longer be moved and inspired by greatness (or worse, don't know it when you see it), it's time to pack it up. If you can't marvel at the beauty of Yosemite Valley or of K. D. Lang and Roy Orbison singing "Crying," if you aren't humbled by the west wall of the Lincoln Memorial, aren't buckled by the language of his second inaugural inscribed there, "With malice toward none, with charity for all," you are already dead. When the color guard at the Tomb of the Unknown Soldier or the tones of Yo-Yo Ma's cello no longer speak to you, you can no longer be reached.

There is always something new to be discovered; every year brings a crop of new moments to inspire. Tastes can't remain complacent, eyes need to stay on the horizon. I hope I will always have moments where I can fall in love with new world order—Sacha Baron Cohen creating *Borat* or the rise of EDM.

I feel like I've scored a few points of my own over the years and will continue to do so, but I can only dream of approaching the transcendent moments of my fellow actors. Of George Scott in *Patton*: "God help me, I do love it so." Streep in *Out of Africa* (off camera, in *voice-over* no less!): "He was not ours, he was not mine." Of Redford in *The Natural*: "I love this game." Of Bill Holden in *Network*: "Because I'm closer to the end than I am to the beginning." Of Streisand when she first sees Hubbell in *The Way We Were*. Of Ray Liotta in *Goodfel-las*: "I'm not going to jail, Karen! Ya know who goes to jail . . . ?" Of the greatest of all time, Paul Newman, in his closing argument in *The Verdict*. Of Daniel Day-Lewis abandoning his boy in *There Will Be Blood* and Demi's single tear in *Ghost*.

Most of us, the 99 percent of us, will never, ever, even come close. But my heroes keep me wanting to try.

Finally meeting my hero, Robert Redford, at the 2014 Golden Globes,
where we were both nominated.

Rehab

As I remember it, my first taste of alcohol came at the hands of my father, somewhere around the age of five. I'm confident on the timing, as he and my mom were no longer in the same rooms beyond that age. But I can clearly see them, in our living room on Aberdeen Avenue in Dayton, setting up for what was probably a fondue party. I was ready for bed in my feetsy pajamas, baby blue, with a teddy bear logo. I probably wanted a sip of whatever it was Dad was holding. I'm fairly positive I knew it wasn't a "pop," as we called soda, or a glass of milk with ice, which was the drink we usually shared on hot summer nights watching the lightning bugs from the screened-in porch.

It was beer, probably Stroh's, as a few years later, that brand would become my favorite. In a move that I've come to know says so many things about my temperament, I didn't gingerly explore this new beverage with a dainty sip; I took a full swig. I practically chugged it. Although today I know why, then I did not. I remember it tasting both terrible and amazing. Then I vomited all over our living room floor.

I wonder if my dad remembers any of this. I wonder, too, if maybe this faded moment is similar to the kinds I have now with my own sons, where they are convinced of a story's veracity while I am not. Sometimes my boys tell me tales of our times together when they were small and I have no idea what they are talking about. Sometimes vice versa. It makes me appreciate that we all have our own points of view, dissimilar abilities to see facts clearly and unique personal narratives. And that in the end, one's personal reality is the only one that ever really matters. I remember my last taste of alcohol as well. It was sometime around four A.M. on May 10, 1990.

This is what happened in between, and what is happening now.

Teenage drinking is the bane of my existence. All of them do it, I did to excess and in the living rooms of Europe, it's sanctioned. Everyone copes with underage drinking differently; our societal standards are all over the road. Any college freshman will tell you that it is common knowledge which bars enforce the drinking age and which ones do not. Some parents let their teens drink from time to time; some are as shocked by that concept as they are when their kids get caught doing it in secret anyway. It all seems like a complicated math problem that everyone solves differently, with answers that don't match, most of them being flat-out wrong. Having a sip of beer at five didn't make me abuse booze later in life. Not drinking until you are of legal age doesn't guarantee you won't become a drunk. A drinking career seems to be formed by a mysterious combination of genetics, personality, environment and mind-set.

What is not shrouded in mystery is the fact that I'm an alcoholic. I believe I was one at the fondue party on Aberdeen Avenue. The big, brave gulp of beer? The "See, I can take it!" attention seeking? The early signs were there, as they always are.

When I was fifteen a bunch of pals and I hid out in a friend's basement with a bottle of gin. Only one of us had to be dragged home by his dad. Me. Everyone else got appropriately wasted; I, on the other hand, was an early believer in the adage that if two swigs were perfect, four would be fantastic!

There was also the time when my pals and I road-tripped to San Diego to see Bruce Springsteen and the E Street Band. We piled into my friend Josh's decrepit late-sixties muscle car gone bad, complete with a terribly painted black racing stripe. We shacked up at a shoddy cut-rate motel and broke out the beer. The next thing I knew we were climbing in and out of the windows to the pool area like monkeys. I think we put some furniture in the deep end.

The teen status symbol of the day was a new brand of red-white-and-blue sunglasses called Vuarnets. They were expensive and only the cool, rich kids had them at our high school. Obviously, we wanted them too. In our stupor, someone (not me) came up with the brilliant idea to try to "lift" a pair.

"Yeah, let's dooo it!"

"For sure! Let's go!!"

"Raaaagh!" went the call of the drunk, young and stupid. We were all in a lather.

But the next thing I knew, it was me, not any of my buds, high-tailing it out of the Big 5 sporting goods store with the damn glasses! Fleeing the scene, I ran directly in front of a police car waiting at a light. I might have gone unnoticed but for the salesman chasing me with a baseball bat.

Later, in the pokey, I concocted a convoluted story about being "forced" to nab the glasses by a threatening stranger. (It made perfect sense to me at the time.) A police sketch artist was brought in.

After a grueling session where he grilled me about every detail of the threatening stranger, the sketch artist produced his rendering of the suspect. No one seemed to notice that when I was done describing him, he looked exactly like Clarence Clemons from the cover of Springsteen's *Born to Run*.

The cops, who had more pressing business than a drunken teen shoplifter with a clearly bullshit story, took pity on me. My parents were called and they drove all night to San Diego to pick me up. My grounding lasted longer than any sentence I would've gotten from juvenile court.

I suppose it would be easy to focus on the terrible adolescent decision-making and total lack of impulse control, and I'm sure that's what my parents did. But today I know that none of those admitted shortcomings come into play without my being drunk. And that having a sneaky six-pack didn't lead any of the other guys in our group into trouble. No, that only happens to the one with the *real* problem, or, to put it another way, if ten guys jaywalk, but only one gets caught, he's likely your alcoholic.

But our world is full of folks who have addiction issues and, for one reason or another, never have either the moment of clarity and stop or the life tragedy that forces them to. I see a lot of them, many who are perfectly successful or seemingly so, with their red wine every single night or their martini at the country club, or their joint before every concert or movie. I have no judgments. I have no problem with people having fun and getting blasted if that's the only way they know how to do it. However, I do wonder what greater achievements, what deeper relationships, could have been had without a lifelong relationship with drugs or alcohol. It's obvious to wonder at the what-ifs of the fatalities; I wonder at the what-ifs of those who still function year in and year out.

That's why I am so thankful that my life had stopped functioning by 1990. What cruel descent awaited me for the rest of my days as a recreational abuser? It probably would have been worse than death, a kind of nonlife of unmet expectations, promises unfulfilled, in terms of both my own potential and being the man I wanted to be for those I love. It would have been a slow slide into a smothering malaise of mediocrity and diminishing returns. I'm not sure my addictions would have ever killed me; I wasn't that type. But it easily could have been even more tragic; I would have died on the inside.

I wrote about the road that led me to rehab in my first book, so I don't need to elaborate much here. Also, there's nothing worse than a parade of "crazy partying" war stories that are meant as a sort of mea culpa confession but are really just darkly self-aggrandizing, tawdry tales. I was a world-famous actor, single, in my early twenties, with money, too much free time, a big libido and a drinking problem. I don't think you need F. Scott Fitzgerald to make my story more clear.

I'm really glad it didn't take a family intervention to get me to find help. I've been a part of these over the years and they are always harrowing. For once, reality television gets it right. And if you watch shows like *Intervention* you know all the storytelling tropes. The subject is always freaked out, there are always family members who think the whole idea is bullshit and there are tears and testimonials, some devastatingly eloquent and some unwatchable. It's sort of what you get at a wedding. Or funeral.

The results are usually decidedly mixed. In fact, come to think of it, I've never been part of an intervention that worked. And by that I mean where the subject says, "Thank you. You are right. I need help. Tell me what to do now and I'll do it." Maybe it's because many of the interventions I've been a part of involved fellow actors. Looking back, I'm not sure that hooking Oliver Stone in via conference call would convince anyone to get sober. But I don't run these interventions, I just participate when asked, and the good news is that most of the subjects did eventually get help. The intervention, however ugly and unsuccessful at the time, turned out to be the first small step on a very long road.

I can only suppose that mine would have been no different. Although it probably would have given me something to laugh about today, over two decades later.

"Rob, holding on line three is the director of *St. Elmo's Fire*. He's very worried for you." Can you imagine? Well, in *that* case I'll change my life completely!

Twenty-some years ago, rehabs were different. In fact, most people hearing that word would have thought of an athlete "rehabbing" a sports injury, not a chai-tea-latte-clutching starlet looking to rehab her image. Because there is such a media obsession with the "high and mighty" being laid low by addiction, you see tons of coverage of folks checking into rehab. And in sobriety, as in marriage, the odds are not in your favor. So unfortunately I think there is a sense among some people that maybe recovery doesn't work.

That is simply not true.

Although there are many who get sober through support groups, I could never have taken my first steps without the knowledge I gained in rehab. Like anything in life, you get out what you put in. I gave my all (I knew the stakes), and I came away with tools I use to this day, every day. I saw talented and dedicated counselors lead some very broken people through unimaginable barriers to come out on the other side with the possibility of a new life. To witness it was life-changing. Seeing others face their ugly secrets and inner conflict gave me the courage to do it myself. That's something I will never forget.

One day, in group therapy we turned our attention to our newest arrival at the facility. I will call him Buck to protect his anonymity, and some of his personal descriptions have been altered as well. Buck was a towering, hulking professional athlete. He may have been the largest man I have ever seen up close. Although one of the elite in his field, he secretly had a substance-abuse problem and on the eve of a world championship it caused him to flame out.

For two weeks he sat in our circle of six, including the counselor, silent and remote. Each of us had our time in the barrel, where we would be on the hot seat, facing probing, often deeply uncomfortable questions and exercises designed to get down to our core issues. Mine dealt with broken-family stuff, teen alienation, fame at the age of fifteen and the ensuing craziness. (I dealt with these themes at length in my first book.) Some days I felt like I had discovered a key to why I was the way I was, some days it all felt like nothing but pain and bullshit.

In fact, it was on one of those latter days, probably halfway through my stay, feeling stalled out and doubtful, that Buck began his time in the barrel and I witnessed a human awakening that has inspired me every day for over two decades.

"Buck, why do you think you have a drug problem?" asked Mike, our counselor.

"Dunno. Just do I guess." We waited for more, but Buck was silent.

"What are you looking to get from your stay here?" asked Mike finally.

"I just want to stop."

"Why do you think you can't?"

"Dunno. I'm . . . I'm helpless," said Buck impassively.

"You're a disciplined, world-class athlete. You come from a broken home, poverty. You've made it to the top of your sport. It looks like you can beat anything, if you set your mind to it," said Mike softly, matter-of-factly, looking him in the eye.

"Like I said, I'm helpless."

"Why do you think that is?"

Buck shrugged. For a long time he said nothing. It got uncomfortable. The people-pleasing part of me, the performer who always wants a happy room, wanted to jump into the conversation to cut the tension.

"Felt that way since I can remember. From a little boy," Buck said finally. I studied his face for emotion but if there was any, I didn't see it. The room felt stalled. But none of us were going anywhere, so there was no choice but to stew in the silence together.

Mike tried another track.

"You have a lot of responsibilities, don't you, Buck."

Buck looked away, focusing on the window.

"Lotta family you take care of? People who depend on you?" Mike said, pressing him.

"Yeah," he said finally, turning back to the group. For the first time since he'd arrived, I saw emotion flicker on his giant, Mount Rushmore face. But after a moment the wall was back up; I could see him retreat completely. Mike saw it too.

"Buck, I want to try something with you. An exercise. Would that be okay?"

Buck said nothing but nodded. Mike went to the couch in the corner and retrieved a big, sturdy blanket. He laid it on the floor in front of our group.

"Buck, would you take off your shoes and lie on the blanket?"

He did as he was asked.

"Rob, can you get the lights?" Mike asked me. I had no idea what was happening but from day one at the rehab I'd made a rule to do whatever I was told. I turned out the lights.

The giant man lay on the blanket. "Close your eyes," said Mike. "You don't need to do anything. We'll all just be quiet for a while." Then, "Everyone, why don't we all get down on the floor with Buck."

Slowly, the group of us slid to the floor in the dark, surrounding him like he was the campfire we would tell stories around.

Buck's eyes were closed; he seemed to relax, but his guard was still up, as always.

"Buck, I know how strong you are. You're a big man. Your sport requires you to be tough. I know you take care of business in the arena. I know you have familial responsibilities, a large bunch of people who depend on you to look out for them. But I want to know this: Who takes care of Buck?"

With that, Mike silently motioned to us to close the blanket. His eyes signaled that he wanted us to do as he did, to follow his lead. He wrapped the man in the blanket and we all helped. I pulled the soft, sturdy fabric to the man's barrel chest. All our hands were on him.

"Today we are going to take care of *you*," Mike whispered to him. "Today no one wants anything from you. Today, you just worry about you."

We stayed like that for a while, our hands softly on him, and he began to breathe deeply. A few minutes passed. Then:

"I think it's probably been a long time since anyone picked you up. Since anyone held you," said Mike. He instructed us to get to our feet, each of us holding the blanket underneath Buck.

Together we pulled. We lifted him up.

We began to rock him slowly, back and forth, almost like he was in a hammock or was a baby in a bassinet. Buck was a monolith, maybe 295 pounds or more, but we held him and rocked him, together.

"I want you to think about little Buck. Really go back, and feel what it was like when you weren't big, when you weren't strong. Be that small boy again."

He began to cry. We kept holding him up, wrapped in his blanket, rocking him in the darkness. Soon his body was wracked with almost inhuman-sounding sobs. I wanted to look away, to avoid seeing a man in such pain.

"What's happening?" Mike asked him evenly, softly. He wasn't pushing; in fact he almost sounded like his mind was elsewhere. "What's going on with you right now?"

The big man gasped. He began to moan like an animal.

"Oooh. Ooh. Oh no!" He was agitated now, and we couldn't hold him up in the blanket, so we laid him down gently in the darkness. "Oh God. Oh God!" he exclaimed. He was writhing on the ground but we held him down and caressed him, like a parent would a new-born.

Mike's voice became clear. "Buck. I need you to talk about what you are remembering."

"I— I— Oh God."

"Shh, shh. We're here. It's okay. You can talk to us."

"I couldn't stop them! I had to stop them! But . . . but . . . they—aaaaah."

It was excruciating. We waited, none of us daring to look at each other. Buck heaved and buckled, dissolving into himself. I thought he might be sick.

"Talk to me, Buck," said Mike.

"I, I was left . . . alone . . . with my baby brother. We were all alone. No one was home. My brother and me . . . we . . . we . . . we played out on the street."

He stopped breathing heavily.

"How old is your brother?"

"A baby. Maybe one and a half."

"And how old are you?"

"I'm, I'm four years old."

"It's okay, Buck, keep going."

"Aaaaah. Uh . . . those boys, the big boys, they took him. They took him."

"What do you mean?"

"I was babysitting. But they wanted to put my brother in this box. I didn't want to. They took him . . . Oh my God."

Buck was shaking. His slab of a chest rising up and down like a hydraulic platform.

This time, Mike didn't step in to guide him. Whatever it was that Buck had suppressed, whatever awful memory it was that was struggling to erupt, it would come out on its own. Finally.

"I fought them. They were too big. There were a lot of them. They put my brother into the box right there on the sidewalk. Then . . . then they were rollin' it and jumpin' on it and I said, 'No! Stop!' but they wouldn't stop."

"Buck, what happened to your little brother?" asked Mike.

"They killed him."

We tried not to gasp. I wanted to throw up.

"When they were done messin' with him and that box he wasn't breathing anymore. He died."

Even Mike couldn't speak. Most of us were crying. Buck's knuckles were turning white gripping the blanket.

"No one did nothing. Those kids told everyone he got in there and some kind of accident happened. They told me they'd get me if I told, so I didn't." He began to sob, and I thought he was going to a place so broken that no one could ever come back from it. I looked at Mike, scared.

"Buck, you need to know that you didn't do anything wrong. You didn't kill your brother, a gang of kids did. You were only four years old! There was nothing you could have possibly done. You were helpless and you are still helpless. A four-year-old should never be put in a position to care for a baby. Would you do that to a four-year-old?"

"No."

"So you see how unfair it is. Do you see that?"

"Yes."

"I need you to listen to me: You need to stop punishing yourself. You are not going to carry the shame that belongs to others. I ask you why you do drugs; you say, 'I'm helpless.' You have it backward. You were helpless *then*. Today you've got to forgive yourself for that. You won't ever be sober until you do."

The big man looked at Mike with the eyes of a tired, desperate swimmer accepting an outstretched arm. I didn't know if his breakthrough would be the key we all were working to find, because he was unable to speak. But his eyes were easy to read.

Underneath the sadness, pain and receding shame was an unmistakable glimmer of hope. There is no recovery for anyone without lifting the lid on the pain of the past and letting in the light. Sometimes the pain might seem small to others, and sometimes it can be truly horrifying, like the secret Buck had been keeping. But until you reconcile it, you're doomed.

The day I checked out of rehab, after thirty-one days, we all formed a circle. We said our good-byes and the emotion was thick; we had been to some very painful and very inspirational places together. Emotionally, we had gone into battle, the fight to literally save each other's lives. We knew that statistically speaking, many of us would drink or use again, a significant number of us within the next ninety days. And as much as I had grown to care for and love some of them, as we said our good-byes I thought, "It might be you, 'cause it sure as fuck isn't going to be me."

I was taught that when dealing with addiction, you can use your more flawed characteristics as strengths. I am both super-competitive and prone to selfishness. It's a full-time job for me to subvert these qualities that often don't do me any favors in life. But in sobriety, they have been my strong suit and extremely helpful. I often look around a room at people in recovery and think, "I am going to be the one who stays." And while I know that today is the only day that matters, I hoard my string of sober days like a major-league hitting streak I'm not about to give up. With some divine help, there is no outside influence that is ever going to make me drink. Not you, not anyone. Not anything. Selfish and competitive.

In rehab I learned to love alcoholics and addicts for what we are and what we are not. We truly view things differently from others and that is our curse and blessing. We have characteristics that are uniquely our own. We are the lives of the party, the dreamers, the romantics, the storytellers, the masters of the grand gesture. We are emotional, passionate and capable of a depth of feeling that is usually the source of our problem. (It's no accident that so many of us are drawn to the arts.)

Unfortunately, we can also be heartbreakers of the highest magnitude: frustrating, maddening, confusing and disappointing quicksilvers who flirt with tragedy on a daily basis. There is no one who can inflict unwarranted pain on the ones they love like an alcoholic/ addict in full flower. But in recovery, we learn how to take our daily medicine, which is an honest admission of powerlessness, and we begin to beat back the tide. I started this on May 10, 1990, and it has made all the difference, every day since.

For many years, I kept a page of legal paper folded in my wallet. On my last night in treatment I made a list of the most inspiring things I had witnessed there. I never wanted to forget that bond I felt with those there with me. I wanted to have something to look at to remind me of their inspiration. My list lasted about seven or eight years, tucked between my driver's license and photos of my wife and kids. One day I took it out and it came apart at the folds, in pieces in my hands. It was time to throw it away. I still think of that paper today. I can no longer remember many specifics of the list; the memories of those connections also broke apart over the decades. But I do remember the first entry. I can still see it written in green Sharpie pen, just as I wrote it in the cafeteria, sipping that awful caffeine-free iced tea. To be inspired, to be humbled, to be reminded, I wrote in big block letters:

"#1: REMEMBER BUCK."

With Sheryl, the day I left rehab.

The Lion's Den

Untreated substance abuse is often treated as "cool" and as sort of a counterculture badge of honor, a way of proclaiming, "Look out, dullards, I'm still *dangerous*." Likewise, sobriety is sometimes looked at as a fertile ground for the has-been and those who may have lost their edge. I was always scared of losing mine, and so, with ninety days sober, I got a tattoo to show I was still all about it. However, one of the gifts of recovery is authenticity, finding your true self. Today I know that I don't care so much about being cool, much less edgy. I've seen too many good friends chase that image to the gates of prison, insanity or death. I still like my tattoo, but it means nothing to me now other than being a reminder that I've found my authentic self. And my authentic self is someone who wouldn't get a tattoo.

I am still capable of admiring those who have a well-known proclivity for partying, when warranted. For example, I still love some of the writings of Dr. Hunter S. Thompson. Recently, he posthumously rose in my estimation when I discovered he was the one who came up with the idea for the Don Johnson television series *Nash Bridges*. Clearly Dr. Thompson's well-known reservations about the entertainment industry didn't inoculate him against its charms. *Nash Bridges* brought the world six seasons of Don Johnson wearing vests (years later, in the same time slot, on the same network, another blond cutie named Simon Baker would don the same look on *The Mentalist*), and both Don and Hunter made a mint off of the show's long, successful run.

To my understanding, Dr. Thompson never wanted to, or even attempted to, create another hit show. If there was any doubt that he was an iconoclast, look no further than that. So it makes me love his famous quote about the TV industry even more. The guy went one-for-one, hit a grand slam in the TV world in his only at-bat, and still said this:

"The TV business is uglier than most things. It is normally perceived as some kind of cruel and shallow money trench, a long plastic hallway where thieves and pimps run free and good men die like dogs, for no good reason."

I would only add that television is also, when it is good and people watch, probably the most fulfilling medium to work in today. With movies becoming almost exclusively about little-seen (and low-paying) passion projects or giant, simpleminded, lowest-common-denominator, theme-park-driven cartoon franchises, television is where actors can act and writers can write. Because people watch in their beds and on their couches, without total strangers surrounding them, while they check their Facebook status, the audience feels a much more personal connection to the actors of television than those of movies. I know this because I've been both.

This year I ended my wildly fun and tremendously fulfilling run on *Parks and Recreation*. What started out as a sort of six-episode experiment ended up as a four-year comedy master class.

I had just been told by the network that aired my then-current series *Brothers & Sisters* that they found my character's political story lines boring and that I would now be playing mainly a diaper-changing daddy and pie-cooking partner to the ladies on the show. Which was not exactly what I had signed up for. So we agreed to part while we were in love.

Somehow the folks at NBC found out I was about to become a free agent, as did the brain trust on their critically acclaimed but struggling second-year comedy. A meeting was set up.

Mike Schur and Greg Daniels, who co-created and wrote on *The Office* (respectively), and I spitballed about my coming on board *Parks and Rec*. We hit it off at once. We made each other laugh and I loved the fresh, young, iconoclastic energy of the show. It felt like I was in the bull's-eye of elite, contemporary American comedy.

I joined the show and it got picked up for the next season.

At the beginning, I was still finishing on *Brothers & Sisters* and appearing on *Californication*. To my understanding no one had ever starred concurrently on three different shows on three different net-works at the same time (and in three different genres!). Chris Traeger became a character that people just seemed to love. He was insanely, dementedly positive and his ruination of the word "literally" *literally* led Merriam-Webster to change the official rules on how it could be properly used. My English-teacher mother would not have been happy. Or maybe very happy, come to think of it!

One of the things I try to strive for in my life is diversity with con-sistency. Anyone can have a couple of big years in their line of work; the real deal is being able to survive and have a very long string of good years. I've also learned the hard way (and there is no other way to learn) that to have longevity, you will surely have to endure your share of misfires, to go along with hits like *Parks and Rec* or my most recent, *Killing Kennedy*.

I've had a few of those along the way.

After the success of *The West Wing* and my departure from it, I was in the enviable position of being the guy people wanted to anchor their new shows. There was an amount of speculation about what my next career move would be, and I had no idea myself. I did know that I didn't want to wait; I wanted to leap back into television soon, and in the best way possible. I've never been one to be a follower; conventional wisdom held that after a long run on a hit, you sat out at least a season before coming back on a show. But that felt arbitrary to me; I had interesting opportunities and love working. Why wait? (Sidebar: In the years since, actors routinely jump right back into the fray, some doing more than one series a year. The world moves too quickly and there is too much competition and not enough attention span in the zeitgeist to demur.)

Television is the most cyclical of businesses, and at the moment drama was king. It seemed to be the golden age of network drama. *ER*, *Law and Order*, *CSI*, *24* and *The West Wing* dominated the ratings and were creative, groundbreaking, buzzed-about hits. It's hard to imagine today, when all the great dramas are on cable, but there was a time.

I had learned so much on *The West Wing*, from how a great show should and shouldn't be run, to how to cast great actors, to the complications of studio–network politics. It was time for me to do my own show. I would produce it and star; I would be in the trenches from start to finish. But first I had to find the right concept.

I read every script around: shows about helicopter medics, airport security personnel, homeland security, spies and suburban family drama. Some were good, some were bad, but most, like all "pilots," were in the middle, in that danger zone where it has equal possibilities to end up a huge hit or a huge bomb. Rarely, if ever, do you get a script where it's a no-brainer. It's always a gamble to be won and lost in a multitude of conscious choices and unforeseen, uncontrollable acts of fate. It's Vegas at its worst, and with higher stakes.

One afternoon I read a script for a show about an idealistic lawyer caught up in a web of moral ambivalence and conspiracy.

My father is a lawyer and my character on *The West Wing* was recruited out of a big law firm to the White House, so I knew my way around that world. I liked it and it spoke to me. It felt authentic, which is nonnegotiable when developing a show concept. NBC was looking to find a traditional legal drama and would put the show on the air if I was interested. At the time NBC was the best network on TV and felt like home after so many years on *The West Wing*. So I read *The Lyon's Den* and jumped on board.

The "Lyon" of the title was a play on the law firm's name of Lyons, LaCross and Lavine. By the end of my experience working on the show, it would be less cute wordplay than a literal description of the life (and death) of this particular show.

The concept of the series was this: My character, Jack Turner, was plucked from his free law clinic and brought to the white-shoe firm of Lyons and LaCross after the mysterious death of his mentor Dan Barrington, who ran the place. Owing it to his memory, Jack leaves the world of street law and involves himself in high-stakes cases as he becomes increasingly convinced his mentor was murdered, possibly because of something or someone at the firm.

We set out to find a cast of great actors. I read with everyone we saw, culled the field down to two or three finalists for each role and selected them to bring before the studio and, if they survived the cut, the network. Studios and networks have their own mysterious matrix for choosing actors, but my criteria were clear (and remain the same today). I want actors who can actually act, I don't want everyone to look like a model, I don't care if they are "old" or "young," I am not interested in skin color of any hue, I would prefer if they knew their way around a joke when needed and above all they have to have charisma. This has *nothing* to do with physical appearance and is unfortunately and surprisingly a matter of taste. There are "stars" whom I wouldn't watch if they took off all their clothes and self-immolated on the commissary steps, and yet many seem to love them. I wanted actors who I thought had the possibility of "breaking out," as we say in industry-speak, meaning: I wanted people who could be stars on their own shows someday.

Our final cast was: Kyle Chandler, Elizabeth Mitchell, David Krumholtz, Matt Craven and James Pickens Jr. Eventually they *would* carry their own hit shows, *Friday Night Lights, Lost, Numb3rs, Resurrection* and *Grey's Anatomy*, respectively. It was a stellar group, and we were lucky to have them.

We shot the first script and all was well. The network liked it enough to give us the coveted ten P.M. Sunday slot, or "beachfront property," as they say. The legendary former head of NBC Warren Littlefield stopped me at lunch one day and called *The Lyon's Den* "the pride of the fleet."

But so was the *Bismarck*.

Our airdate was set for September 28, 2003. By that time we would already have six episodes in the can. So there would be no ability to write to the audience's interests or to minimize elements of the show that people were less interested in.

When I read our second script I knew we had trouble. The mystery of who killed my mentor at the firm was now even more confusing and muddled. The cases I was involved in were not as exciting as I had hoped and there was little tension in a show that professed to be a thriller. Desperate, I sat in the same chair for twenty-four straight hours and rewrote, gave thoughts and made suggestions, but neither the studio nor the network seemed as worried as I was about the writing. Each week, my instincts continued to catch fire. Soon, as one of the show's executive producers, I urged my bosses at the studio to make a change before it was too late. They too thought the storytelling could be improved but were unwilling to replace the head writer; it would be too expensive and send a message that this big, shiny new show was already in trouble.

Weeks later, they would finally act, but it would be too little too late. And it is a great lesson: Creative issues do not magically sort themselves out; nine times out of ten, they only get worse. If you feel like a change is necessary, do it early. No one gives you brownie points for patience, and you don't get extra Nielsen ratings for misplaced loyalty.

As our premiere date approached, few appreciated that we were then in the final years of the era of big network ratings. The rise of cable series and the allure of the Internet and DVRs were just beginning to erode the giant numbers everyone was accustomed to. Unfortunately for *The Lyon's Den*, NBC was still judging ratings by standards that had changed and expecting numbers that would never again be at the levels of the recent past.

On premiere night we drew ten million viewers for a 3.4/9 share in the coveted eighteen-to-twenty-nine-year-old demo. Today, that would make us a big top-ten hit, but then it was considered a "soft" opening.

On the day before our debut, I couldn't get anyone to talk about improving our show. The day after, the studio and network were crawling all over us to "fix" the series.

Finally! I was all ears.

The brass wanted to write a four-episode arc about an opposing lawyer with whom I would fall in love. It sounded great to me. I wanted to cast someone unexpected, not just a "hot" actress. I had seen the Ang Lee movie *Ride with the Devil* and liked the performance of Jewel, the singer/songwriter.

The network and studio were dubious at best. Jewel's personal narrative was well-known; she was a country gal from Alaska who grew up using an outhouse.

"Why would we believe her as an Ivy League, top-gun, big-city attorney?" I was asked by one of the executives.

"Trust me. She's talented, she's interesting, it's a cool choice. And if she's good enough for Ang Lee, she's good enough for us!" Using all of my goodwill and capital with the studio and the network, I got Jewel the job.

But there was a hiccup.

Jewel, it turned out, wasn't sure she wanted the part. I was enlisted to cajole her on a phone call.

"Do you really want to do more acting?" I asked her.

"Yes," she said.

"Well, this could be the type of part that people will notice *and* it's outside of anything you've done. You will have complicated, sophisticated dialogue, play a Harvard grad, wear beautiful, classic, sexy, modern businesswoman wardrobe—it will be as far away from 'country' as it gets! And that's what acting should be. Moving out of what you are known for."

"Will there be an audience?"

"Um, no," I explained, "this isn't a sitcom. It's a traditional drama, it's not shot live or anything."

"Oh, too bad. I like audiences."

We had a nice chat and by the time she asked if she could read me some poetry, she seemed to be excited to do the part.

As an attempt to be closer to my family, I had, as part of my contract, a stipulation that the show would be shot at a studio in the San Fernando Valley, a good forty-five minutes closer than the studios in Hollywood proper. But to save costs, instead of shooting at Warner Bros., Universal or any of the other lots, a paint-thinning plant in an industrial area of the Valley was retrofitted for us. Sometimes in the late-fall San Fernando heat, it would be one hundred degrees on our jerry-rigged "soundstage," and people would faint from the paint fumes. Pornos were shot in the same industrial park and directly next door was a bustling dildo factory. As our ratings continued to slip, shooting in this porno-paint hinterland didn't help anyone's confidence or mood.

Each day, in spite of being in almost every scene, I found myself in an emergency triage of some sort: meetings on future stories, casting sessions, talking to local affiliates and doing the press that drives a show. It got to the point where acting in the show was considered an afterthought, and I hated that. On most series, the head writer, or "show runner," would handle these tasks, but not on this one. He was a first-timer, timid by nature, probably overwhelmed. He was also very involved in a drastic diet, which, he proudly told anyone who would listen, was "for the Emmys." Having been to the Emmys, and won, four years in a row with my last show, I didn't know how to tell him that we were not likely to need our tuxedos. At least not yet.

I began to understand that our show was not "bad" by any standard; in fact, it was among the smarter and more well-made dramas on any network. But it lacked a constant point of view, moved too slowly, was good-but-not-great and was damned by that. If it had been clearly inferior, there would have been a will to fix it.

Back at the paint-thinning plant, the Jewel experiment had promising early results. She was, as I had hoped, sort of extraordinary in her pencil skirts, rattling off sassy legalese in our scenes where we would spar and flirt. Everyone was optimistic and for a moment, our show felt ascendant.

Then came the love scene.

The sequence seemed to surprise her, which made little sense since the scene wasn't new or a rewrite; it had always been in the script, which I could only hope and assume she had actually read previously.

But for whatever reason, on the day of the shoot, things were different. For the first time, she brought her boyfriend to the set. It was great for me; I'm a huge sports fan and he was an iconic rodeo champion and a really nice guy. I got him a seat at the monitor next to her chair, but she elected to sit on his lap.

By the way, when I say "love scene," I'm not talking about her and I being totally naked like Demi Moore and me in *About Last Night . . .* , or Kim Cattrall in *Masquerade,* or Jodie Foster or Nastassja Kinski in *Hotel New Hampshire.* Those were movies; this was television, and not even cable! How steamy can you be with no nudity and a network censor editing your story lines? In fact, the "love scene" was really just a moment where, fully clothed, in a deserted office late at night, we kissed, then lay down on a desk. And even that part was out of frame.

Jewel didn't want to kiss me. She asked if we could restage the scene without it. We tried it, because you never know what good might come out of another actor's instinct, however bad it may seem. Not surprisingly, it turned out that we needed to kiss to make the scene a "love" scene. Jewel balked and ran to the monitor, where she jumped onto her boyfriend's lap. She began kissing him instead.

I was beginning to take it personally. I checked my breath; it seemed okay to me, but I popped an Altoid just to be safe. The director huddled with both Jewel and her man, trying to get us back on track.

I gave them their space as the crew watched this little drama play out. My mind took the opportunity to work through the laundry list of challenges of the day. There were story pitches to go over, edited footage to look at, an international press junket during lunch and a meeting with our director of photography about tweaking the show's visuals. I checked my watch, worrying about staying on schedule. Someone opened a door somewhere and I smelled the eye-watering, headache-inducing aroma of what I assumed to be the color magenta.

Finally, Jewel and the director made their way back to the set. She didn't seem pleased.

"Let's just do this," she said.

We did the scene and it went well. But as we approached the kissing moment it became strained, and it's never good when you can't trust that your fellow actor is on the same page. I had no idea what this woman would do when I had to kiss her.

The moment arrived.

The script called for a heated, passionate coming together. But it ended up being less *Fifty Shades of Grey* and more *Grey Gardens*. And by that I mean confusing, a little scary and very slow. I pecked her on the lips; her mouth scrunched closed like you would do if someone was going to stick something unwanted into it, which I was not intending.

I sort of moved my head from side to side to make it look real, like there was at least a dollop of energy or passion.

"Cut," said the director.

Jewel looked at me and wiped the back of her hand across her lips like an American Sign Language version of "Yuck."

But at that point it was just another in a long series of breaks that just weren't going my way. The scene, and her whole story line, ended up being a nonevent. And although we had planned to have one of Jewel's beautiful ballads under our love scene, in the end, I used one from Dido instead.

I am an eternal, never-say-die optimist. I will fight to the last man. But I also would never have gotten from the bad neighborhoods of Dayton, Ohio, to where I am now without being able to delude myself when needed. As our ratings failed to improve and signals of our demise were everywhere, I woke up every day convinced that we could turn it around.

My old pal from the eighties, Michael J. Fox, had not done television in over a decade. But one of our best writers, Kevin Falls, whom I imported from *The West Wing*, had pitched a character that was extraordinary. We hoped it might lure Mike to do our show. Now *that* would be a game changer. To my delight, Mike didn't dismiss it out of hand. He had only one request. He wanted to read it by the following week, as he was going out of town and needed to reschedule if he liked the part.

"That's plenty of time. We will write you something great," I said.

A week later there were still no scenes to show Mike. Kevin Falls and I were pulling our hair out, but our head writer was behind closed doors.

"Why don't *you* just write the scenes?" I asked Kevin.

"Can't, that's the head writer's area."

On the last day to get the script to Mike, I went to the production office.

"I need the scene."

"Sorry, he's behind closed doors," said the writer's assistant.

"He's been working on this for *days*!"

"I'm sorry, he can't be disturbed."

I grabbed the door and burst into the office.

The head writer didn't look up from his computer screen; he was wearing headphones. I was stunned to see that instead of dialogue on his screen, there were video images of his kids playing basketball. I realized he was editing home movies.

Michael J. Fox never got his scenes and didn't do our show. But Kevin Falls got promoted to take over all writing duties and overnight, I had hope again. Our stories became crisper; the show's dramatic narrative was refined (we finally got rid of the endless "who killed the mentor" plot) and we made at least one or two episodes that were as good as anything I'd been a part of.

By Halloween, I was so exhausted from the fifteen-hour days, five days a week, plus the long commute from Santa Barbara, that I had a mattress installed in the back of the Suburban that brought me to work. I would crawl in in the morning darkness, still in my pajamas; arrive at sunrise; be plied with three shots of espresso and shower before makeup in my trailer. On the way home I watched the week's footage on a DVD player and caught up on paperwork. I had no time for anything else; I barely saw my family, I left before dawn and I got home as the kids went to sleep. I was a shell.

One day, our route to work was cut off by a giant, raging wildfire that was causing the evacuation of the entire northwestern Valley. All around the hillside of the 118 freeway I could see fifty-foot flames shooting into the graying dawn. It was already hot as hell. It was five thirty in the morning and eighty degrees.

Pulling up to our industrial complex, there was chaos at the dildo factory. An unsettling-looking group scurried to prepare for what I was now told was "imminent evacuations." But at *The Lyon's Den*, we knew we had no such option. We would shoot regardless. The guys who make dildos may get to run for safety, but those who make television do not.

Due to the extreme heat, our air conditioners, which were rudimentary anyway, failed by noon. The temperature on the set stood at 103 degrees. The paint fumes in that kind of heat were making some on the crew faint. The noise of firefighting helicopters and fire engines made shooting almost impossible.

Around three o'clock, I received an urgent summons to the production offices. I put the cast and crew on a ten-minute break and weaved my way through the prefab hallways and other elements of the set to the main offices. Stepping outside, I saw that the fire was roaring down from the hills a few miles away. "Perfect metaphor for this show," I remember thinking.

The president of NBC was holding and wanted Kevin Falls and me on the line ASAP. Settling in to pick up the call, we hoped he was calling to congratulate us on a particular story line he had personally requested, which we had added into an episode in record time. But looking out the office's windows at a stream of emergency crews rushing to the advancing inferno, even the eternal optimist knew the writing was on the wall.

"Sorry, guys, we're pulling the show," he said immediately, the moment we picked up. And that was that. After airing six episodes, *The Lyon's Den* was done. Although not officially canceled. No one in television uses that phrase anymore. Shows aren't canceled these days, they are "off the schedule" or "on hiatus" or "pulled." It's absurd because everyone knows when a show is dead no matter what new, feel-good, never-admit-a-failure buzz-speak you use. It's like asking your vet, "Did my cat survive his operation?" and being told, "Well, his vital signs are currently on hiatus."

Regardless, the studio that financed *The Lyon's Den* for NBC wanted us to shoot our contractually obligated thirteen-episode order, even though they would never be aired. The theory was that money might still be made on DVDs or in foreign markets. This is a pretty rare occurrence and a real character builder. It is not easy to get it up for fourteen-hour days working on a canceled TV show.

All my life, and still today, I've pushed through negativity, setbacks, bad reviews, poor ratings and breaks going against me whenever I've had to. As the ominous signs piled up on *The Lyon's Den* I herniated myself trying to find a silver lining. I worked to the final moment and hoped against hope that there might be a turnaround. I kept waiting for the trend to reverse. And I also never lost sight of the fact that through hard work and God's grace, I live a very blessed life. A failed TV show is the very definition of a first-world problem.

The cast and crew took the news as well as could be expected. We had become close, as one does when you are under fire. I shared with them a new lesson I had learned from my experiences on everything from successes like *Wayne's World* and *The West Wing* to projects that didn't work out: "Sometimes there is absolutely nothing you can do to stop something from being a hit and sometimes there is absolutely nothing you can do to stop something from being a flop." The show-business gods cannot be manipulated. It is both the good news and bad news of our line of work.

But there was worse to come.

Shortly after our cancelation, my mother passed away at sixty-four, from her battle with breast cancer. It happened on a weekend; my wife, my brother Micah and I were with her till the end. I went to work Monday; my producing partners and the studio asked if I wanted time off, but the show would've shut down without me. I wrote my mother's eulogy on the set between scenes. I would like to think she would've been proud of that.

All things end. They rarely end as we would like them to and often do so before we are ready. We transition in a way that gives our loss honor; we grieve with a love and true appreciation for what we have no longer. It was clear that my mom was ready to go; it was her time. My love of her and my desperation to keep her in my life were of no consequence to that fact, any more than my relentless attempts to improve *The Lyon's Den* kept it from cancellation. Both personally and professionally I was swamped with the message: Your plan pales compared to the larger one.

We laid my mother to rest under a shading oak on a sweltering afternoon in Santa Barbara. The turnout for her was huge and I was overcome by the support of so many friends. When my sons spoke to the packed church at eight and ten years old, dressed in their tiny suits, it was one of the proudest moments of my life.

Back on the set, we still had a number of episodes to shoot and scripts to write. Since *The Lyon's Den* was a "dead" show, no one from the network or studio was mandating our story lines. We had complete freedom. "What should we do with the remaining episodes? How should we end the series?" Kevin Falls asked me.

"Let's go out strong. Let's be daring. Let's burn all the bridges," I said.

So in the end, we built to a finale that *no one* would see coming. We decided to blow people's minds. (Not that anyone would see it, unless they lived in some foreign hinterland where they air failed shows.) We decided that my character, the hero of *The Lyon's Den*, would be revealed as a psychopathic schizophrenic who was, in fact, the murderer of his mentor. To their credit, when we shared this outrageous finale with the studio, they said, "Hey, whatever you guys want!"

So on the last day, we shot the last scene of the script. It took place in the law office's big conference room late at night. I sat eating a steak as I invited my office rival, the future coach of *Friday Night Lights*, Kyle Chandler, to a final showdown. In it, he confronted me about secretly being on antipsychotic meds and my involvement in my mentor's death. I walked toward him with a smile, blithely confessed to murder, then stabbed him to death with my steak knife. I then finished my meal, walked to the office balcony and committed suicide by throwing myself off. End of series.

For some reason, I've never seen these final episodes. Every once in a while I'll get a fan letter from Slovakia or Azerbaijan from someone who has. "I saw the ending of *The Lyon's Den*! Jesus Christ! It was insane! You must be crazy!" I usually write back, "No, the TV business is crazy, I'm just learning as I go."

The cast of the *Lyon's Den* (*from left,* Frances Fisher, James Pickens Jr., Matt Craven, me, Kyle Chandler, Elizabeth Mitchell, David Krumholtz).

With my character's would-be love interest, Jewel.

The Mansion

Being eighteen and a freshly minted movie star, only a few years away from Dayton, Ohio, was a mixed bag. On one hand my life's goal was coming into focus, but I was having to navigate some fast-moving waters in Hollywood. And, like any male eighteen-year-old, the most pressing developmental issue I had to face was sex and romance, and how they fit into my life.

I had my first crush in the first grade but got talked out of it by my friends who thought the girl was not up to their seven-year-old standards. By the time I was fifteen I had struggled through the challenge of my peers thinking I was a "theater fag" because I wanted to be an actor and finally found my first serious girlfriend. As my career began to really take off, that relationship began to end, a casualty of immaturity, jealousy and the first blush of fame. By the time my other friends were out of the house for the first time, I was on locations making movies or pounding the pavement in Hollywood, building my career in earnest. And like all young men, it was during those years that I explored all I could about love, relationships, sex and the connections between the three. Of all the "personal discovery" journeys I've been on, this one was clearly the most fun.

Helping matters greatly was the time line: It was pre-AIDS and before the lessons of recreational drug use taught us that cocaine was not an appropriate status symbol. It was also in the time before everyone had a cell phone with a camera attached, before the Internet and Facebook and a culture where everyone simply *has* to post every photo of every party they attend. Although there was the *National Enquirer* and *Star* (then a true tabloid and not a celeb-photo book), there was no TMZ or Radar, no Perez Hilton or any of today's myriad of pay-for-play gossip sites. There were no armies of paparazzi staked out in my beloved Malibu or on Rodeo Drive or at LAX or any of the cool restaurants or clubs. There were no "Stars Are Just Like Us!"/"Baby Bump Watch!" banal and reductive celeb editorializations in the "straight" media. It wouldn't have been tolerated, either by the public or on the streets at the clubs or restaurants. But then again, the cover boys of that era were Beatty, Newman and Redford. Instead of couples from *Dancing with the Stars*, we had Jack Nicholson and Anjelica Huston. It was a *totally* different era in terms of what we valued. The net effect was this: We were more innocent and trusting, and there was actually some privacy and decorum, but with plenty of room to get wild, if the opportunity arose.

It was also before the two events that irreparably damaged one of the great bastions of the sexual revolution, the Playboy Mansion. Internet porn killed the business model and reality TV killed the Bunnies. With the possible exception of becoming a Laker Girl (today also devoid of its status), back then, if you were a gorgeous, marginally talented young woman, becoming a Bunny was one of your only shots at fame. Not anymore. Today, if you are willing to eat bugs or throw a chair at your best friend or mother, you can star in a reality TV series.

The Playboy Mansion of the early to mideighties was a thing to behold. Sure, even as a nineteen-year-old, I knew it was on a slide from its heyday. But to have been there in the seventies when Hef was young, the pill was new and James Caan *lived there* would have been too much to handle. I barely survived my first-time visit as it was!

An invitation to come to the mansion for movie night was a tough ticket to get. You couldn't buy your way in; you couldn't use connections or a publicist or any Hollywood lever pulling. Invitations came directly from Hugh Hefner, and he cast his parties very carefully in those days. In his magazine, the *Playboy* interview was *the* most insightful, dangerous, prestigious and coveted profile in all media, so there was a patina of intellectual exclusiveness almost as strong as the sexual undercurrent associated with Hef's gatherings. The crowd could vary from screenwriting geniuses like Robert Towne and Buck Henry to star athletes like Magic Johnson. It goes without saying that you would also see the absolute top tier of beautiful and usually available women that LA had to offer. That they were comprised of the top lookers of a wide range of American cities effectively made them among the most stunning groups of women in the country.

I had just finished *The Outsiders* when I got a call from "Mr. Hefner's" office inviting me to a Super Bowl party. I was specifically told that I could not bring a guest and I was required (for reasons I never understood) to provide my driver's license number and a description of the car I would be driving.

I was the envy of all my pals. My friends from my school days in Malibu always enjoyed the collateral of my new life in the movies, but the *Playboy Mansion*! Are you kidding me?! We had visions of God only knows what streaming through our heads. Of course they were bummed that they couldn't come with me.

"I will go it alone," I said solemnly.

On game day I arrived at the mansion's massive gates on Charing

Cross Road in Holmby Hills, an even more exclusive area than Beverly Hills, if you can imagine. Sitting in my first car, a white Mazda 626, I waited to be let in. After a moment, I heard a voice.

"Can I help you?"

I rolled down my window and looked around; no one was there. Very strange.

"Hello! Can I help you?" it said again, and I realized it was coming from inside of a giant granite rock. Looking closer, I discovered a speaker chiseled into its face.

"Oh, hi. I'm Rob Lowe. I'm here for the Super Bowl party," I said, trying to seem nonchalant.

The gates swung open.

I drove up the long, winding driveway to a large house that looked like Wayne Manor from *Batman*. The motor court was filled with Porsches, Mercedes and a lime-green Ferrari. I hadn't set foot inside and already I was feeling "less than."

This wasn't a new sensation for me, because until I got famous, I hadn't had a great romantic career. I always loved girls, even in grade school. That did me no favors with the guys, who thought girls were lame, or with the girls, who clearly thought I was some moony-eyed dweeb. Then in middle school I had the misfortune of having the dream of being an actor, which, again, the guys hated and gave me no juice with the girls, who were only interested in the volleyball players and surfers. By the time high school rolled around, like any kid of that age, my sexual self-image was cast. I was not in the cool set, and no "it" girl would give me the time of day; I wasn't an abject loser—I had a few girls who liked me fine—but I was clearly never going to play in the big leagues, like many of the guys strutting around the high school quad.

I've heard that fame doesn't change you so much as it changes the people around you. It was certainly true for me. Stepping out of my little Mazda at the Playboy Mansion, I was only a year and a half beyond not being a part of the cool parties and being totally ignored by 90 percent of the girls I thought were attractive.

Yet here I was, invited into the inner sanctum of Hugh Hefner, one of the twentieth century's arbiters of cool as well as the undisputed king ladies' man. The career .190 hitter was getting his first start in the bigs.

A butler held the heavy, Gothic-style door open as I entered the large stone-floored foyer. Tudor wood-paneled walls and a staircase to my left. A bustling bar right in front of me, where maybe twenty or so people mingled. There was no one to greet me; I knew no one and didn't recognize any of the folks chatting and drinking. If there were cool celebs around, like Mick Jagger or Jack Nicholson, I certainly didn't see them. I scanned the foyer for someone to talk to. The crowd was older than I was, most by about at least a decade, some by three or four.

"Where are the Bunnies?" I thought. I was surrounded by men who looked like either doctors or rock star managers. I made my way to the bar and ordered my traditional starter, a Corona with lime. Like any good alcoholic in the making, I downed it. Sipping was a talent I neither possessed nor admired.

"I'll have another," I said, and the bartender, who had probably seen a number of my kind, never batted an eye. Slowly, I felt the edge being taken off and I began to relax, the booze giving me both comfort and confidence.

"Where are the Bunnies?!"

I noticed people coming in and out of a darkened archway to the right. I made my way over and saw that it led to a screening room. The only light came from its Cineplex-sized screen, which was showing the opening coin toss of the game. It was enough light to glimpse the crowd; sitting on rows of couches I saw mostly middle-aged guys, a few familiar older television actors and their dates, none of whom appeared to be Bunnies.

I felt a hand on my shoulder.

"Glad you could make it." It was Hugh Hefner. In silk pajamas.

What if Babe Ruth wore nothing but pinstripes all the time? What if Kobe Bryant never took off his Lakers jersey or Bruce Springsteen still wore his *Born in the USA* headband? Imagine meeting Tiger Woods in his Sunday red and black or seeing Robert Downey Jr. in his Iron Man suit at lunch in the Polo Lounge. It's one thing to meet a celebrity; it is something else to meet them in their most iconic form in everyday life. You almost believe it's some sort of send-up. But Hef in PJs at midday in the middle of a party seemed totally organic.

I managed a few words, thanking him for the invitation.

"Well, make yourself at home. Have a good time," he said, heading back to the screening room holding his beloved can of Coke. There were no empty seats in the theater to watch the game, so I decided to explore.

The mansion's grounds were lush and vast, with pathways leading to topiaries, past manicured lawns and through koi ponds and cages with monkeys shrieking. Eventually I heard the sounds of the Super Bowl coming from a small dollhouselike cottage nestled among towering stone pines. The door was ajar. From inside came the sounds of girls giggling and talking.

"Hello! Hello!" I called, peeking in. "Does anyone know the score?"

It was the mother lode. There must have been five or six *Playboy* centerfolds splayed about the cozy den, wearing very provocative and skimpy outfits.

"Oh, hiiii!" they cooed, and I knew at once that they'd clearly seen and liked *The Outsiders*.

"I don't mean to interrupt."

"Come in here!" one of them demanded, pointing to a chaise lounge she was lying on.

"Yeah, stay with us! We're *so* bored," said another.

I felt like I had wandered into a fantastic secret world where no men existed but me and the entire female race was comprised of doe-eyed, well-endowed beauties who seemed to *really* need company. It was a long way from the quad at Santa Monica High School, with not a surfer or volleyball stud to be found. I guess these gals would have to make do with me.

I felt like a pharaoh or, I suppose, a junior Hugh Hefner. The girls poured me drinks, laughed, flirted, ran their fingers through my hair and generally seemed to be having as much fun toying with me as they possibly could. In an added bonus, they were sophisticated sports fans.

"I bet they don't beat the spread," said the blond.

Soon enough, one of my adolescent fantasies was realized when one of the Playmates dragged me into her guest room.

When I finally staggered out of the little Hansel and Gretel cottage in the pines, I was both elated and disoriented. Could this possibly be what it was like all the time up here? Had this even really happened? I made myself presentable and made my way back to the party.

The game was long over as I headed back to the main house. The sun had set, and in the moonlight the vibe had shifted considerably. Now girls were everywhere and the middle-aged doctors and music-biz honchos chatted them up in dimly lit corners. An Academy Award–winning writer held court on the patio.

I found myself talking to a well-put-together man in his late forties.

"What do you do?" I asked.

"I do all the work up here," he replied.

"Do you build or just manage the property?" I asked.

He laughed. "No, no. I do all the *work* up here. For *Playboy*," he said, as if I should get his meaning. He stared at me like I was a moron.

"I'm a *surgeon*," he said finally.

"Oh, you're a . . . plastic surgeon?"

"Ex-actly," he said, making a small toasting motion. "Also do all Michael's work."

"Aaaaah," I said sagely, knowing of only one Michael synonymous with plastic surgery. "Yes, I've seen your efforts."

"Here's my card. If you need anything." He smiled, heading off to a very large-breasted woman nearby, probably for some sort of inspection or warranty check.

My Hansel-and-Gretel-house Playmate and I had made a plan to rendezvous for a Jacuzzi in the famous "Grotto" I had heard so much about, so I began to make my way across the giant backyard to the pool. To my infinite happiness, yet another bar was set up on the lawn. With the evening drawing to a close, I shifted to my main drink, a vodka tonic. (In those days I paid an inordinate amount of attention to finding the perfect level of artificially induced "happy feelings." I used them like a suit of armor. And let's face it, like most guys my age, I loved a free bar.) Drink in hand, I explored the pool area.

I had heard stories that the Grotto had underwater tunnels, Jacuzzis and secret chambers. This sounded so cool to me and not unlike a scaled-down version of the backyard pool at Martin Sheen's house. (Sans Playmates, obviously!) Like Indiana Jones, I noted the large waterfall, which is always a dead giveaway of a secret chamber behind it. Sure enough, as I walked around the faux cliff face it cascaded over, I discovered a discreet stone passageway.

I peeked inside.

I discovered a steaming, humid, dimly lit cavern that looked like something out of *The Land of the Lost*. One large body of water surrounded by other walled-off Jacuzzis shimmered behind the back face of the waterfall, which kept the little cave totally blocked from any vantage point on the property. Sometimes the steam grew so thick that it was hard to see more than a yard ahead.

My new friend had told me to go into the dressing rooms and change, and eventually I found one of the numbered rooms and did so. I didn't have the guts (or any other piece of anatomy I may have needed) to go au naturel. I waded into the bathtub-temperature water in my boxers.

Hidden speakers played an obscure cut from *Emotional Rescue* by the Stones. I looked around for my Playmate friend, but she was clearly running late. After some moments contemplating the uniqueness of my surroundings, I began to hear gentle splashing coming from the other side of the Grotto. The steam prevented me from being able to see anything as I made my way toward the sound.

I began to see the outline of a girl silhouetted in the shadows and the reflections coming off the water.

"Hi there! Who is that? Come closer so I can see you," she said. (It was not the voice of my Hansel-and-Gretel Playmate.)

Being no idiot, I did as I was told. She was standing, facing me, leaning on her elbows on the other side of the wall that divided the pool I was in from the tiny Jacuzzi she was in. The added heat made it almost impossible to see through the rising steam. Even though I was right in front of her, it took me a moment to see that she was naked.

"Hi," I managed to say.

"Hi back," she said, and winked at me.

Oh jeez. I didn't know what the correct move was. There was still no sign of the girl I was supposed to meet.

"Have I seen you before?" she asked.

"No, this is my first time at the mansion."

"Are you an actor or something?"

"I am. I'm just getting started. I'm in the movie *The Outsiders.*"

"Ooooooaaaaaaggggmpph," she grunted, making a pained expression.

"Yes, I was a little disappointed in the film myself," I said. "A lot of my stuff is on the cutting room floor."

"Aw, that's too bad. You seem so nice," she replied.

As I tried to figure out the connection between my being "nice" and being cut from the film, she grunted again.

"Aaaaaggggh!" Her head lolled to the side and I wondered if perhaps she was having a medical episode. I looked around for my tardy date or maybe an emergency technician in case she slipped below the bubbling water, but she made a fast recovery. "I think acting is hard. People think it's fun and easy, but it's not. Not from what I can see," she said. Her smile was sweet and kind. I tried to focus on her face and not her breasts.

"So . . . do . . . you get up here often?" I asked.

"I live here."

"Wow, what's that like?" I asked.

"Sorta like being in a sorority. I think."

"I can see that," I said, enjoying my casual conversation with a naked Bunny in the grotto.

"I like it. It's fun. I . . . aaaooooh! Mmmmmaaaah!" she suddenly exclaimed as her big blue eyes rolled up in her head.

And then I saw it.

The steam shifted slightly to reveal a tree-trunk-sized ebony arm wrapped around her waist from behind.

She began to moan. "Oooooh! Yeaaaauuuooow!"

Peering closer, I recognized the man behind her as a legendary Hall of Fame football star. I locked eyes with him, embarrassed.

"Hey, man," he rumbled with a tiny nod and without a care in the world. I nodded politely back.

"Um . . . well, nice meeting you!" I said to the girl.

"You too!" she said, sweet as pie.

"And you as well . . . sir," I said, backing away quickly but with as much dignity as possible.

"Uuuuuuurrrgh!" she said, enveloped in the mist.

Later, driving home in my car, I attempted to make sense of my night at the mansion. Replaying images that would stay with me for years, I realized I had been stood up in the Grotto and I'd never found out who won the Super Bowl. Should've asked the dude in the Jacuzzi.

Threesome! A few years later, back at the mansion with Hef and Mel Brooks. Brooks clearly didn't understand the dress code.

Wish Sandwich

My youngest son, Johnowen, was born with asthma and some serious allergies. Although he's outgrown them now, when he was a little boy it was a serious issue for us. The battery of daily medications made him small for his age at the time and although he loved sports, he was never the strongest or biggest on his teams. Nevertheless, he played with a passion and enjoyed flag football, baseball and basketball as well as tae kwon do.

I loved watching my boys play sports. Maybe it's because I was always picked last (as the theater nerd) that I had such pride and satisfaction watching them. I loved coaching them. It was another way to be close to them. It was also the best way I knew to be just like any other father in America. It was about them, not me, *us*, not anyone else, and had nothing at all to do with the complications of my professional life. I could disappear into two things I love very much, my sons and sports. And it kept show business in its proper perspective, as the *other* thing I did, when the games were done and the boys were showered and comfortable back at home.

After the passing of my mother and the cancellation of *The Lyon's Den*, I spent my free time as the coach of Johnowen's YMCA baseball team. The league was "coach pitch" and that was great. I was able to actually be a part of the game as I threw strikes for the little guys to hit. I became fixated on my team. I spent more of my time setting lineups than reading incoming scripts. This world of exuberant boys felt safer and more rewarding than returning to the currents of Hollywood.

One day we played the best team in the league. They were bigger, stronger and faster than us and were led by the champion golfer Fred Couples's son, who could crush the ball a mile, at will, just like his old man. Going into our game against them, they were undefeated.

By the third inning we were getting our hats handed to us. One of the reasons was the play of their first baseman. The kid was gargantuan, a Sasquatch of a boy. I'm surprised they were able to get a uniform big enough to fit him. Whenever there was a play at first, he would stand in the baseline, forcing our guys to run around him to reach the bag. No one did. In fact, a lot of my boys were so intimidated by this hulk that they just stopped in front of him and were inevitably tagged out.

"Um, hey, it's illegal for the first baseman to block the base runner," I reminded the umpire.

"Yeah, I know, but these kids are just learning the rules," he replied tartly, as if I'd just asked him to toss the kid out of the game.

"I totally get it. But what he's doing is against the rules; let's teach him." The ump grunted and went over to talk to the opposing coach.

When play resumed the same thing happened. This time it was Johnowen at the bat, who hit a ball to the shortstop and headed to first. Once again, the kid stepped in front of Johnowen, who, faced with a player three times his size, stopped in his tracks. The ball was thrown to first and he was called out where he stood.

I was seething.

"Time!" I called.

I got the team into a huddle.

"All right, guys. Listen up. What that player is doing is illegal. He is trying to stop you from running to first. I've told the ump that he needs to get out of the way. If he does it again I want you to run him over."

The kids looked at me with big eyes.

"Knock him on his ass. He's trying to scare you with his size."

The boys nodded, but I could tell they were less than enthusiastic.

The game resumed and for the next few innings there were no plays at first.

Then, Johnowen hit a dribbler to the pitcher. The boy fumbled it as Johnny ran down the line to first. As usual, the human shield moved into his way. The pitcher made the throw; it was going to be close.

Then, my asthma-challenged son, the tiniest kid on the field, lowered his little body and dove headfirst driving his shoulder into the gut of their towering first baseman. The kid flew backward. The ball sailed over his head. Both players went flying to the ground. Johnowen crawled to the base as the ball rolled around the infield.

"Safe!" yelled the umpire.

Our team exploded. Kids were jumping up and down cheering. Johnowen sat on the bag catching his breath. I wanted to run to him, fearing he may have hurt himself, but something told me not to. Instead, I walked over slowly.

"Everyone okay here?" I asked both of them.

"Um, yeah, I'm fine," said the brute. "He ran me over!"

"Looks like it!" I said, heading toward my son.

"Good play," I told him, and patted his back as casually as I could. "Thanks, Dad!" he said, smiling.

We didn't win that day. But on the ride home, you'd never have known.

That night, it occurred to me that if little Johnny could literally throw himself into the game and through his fear, if my tiny team of boys could remain excited and get pumped for the next game after having lost yet another, I needed to do the same in my own life.

Sheryl and I were both big fans of *Nip/Tuck*, a new show on cable that was, at least in its first few seasons, groundbreaking, truly audacious, sexy-smart and wonderfully demented. It was a totally fresh and inspired retrofitting of the classic genre of doctor shows. *Exactly* the kind of show I would have loved to be a part of. A meeting was arranged with the show's creator, Ryan Murphy. I could tell him how obsessed I was with his show and hopefully we'd find something to do together one day. We met for lunch at Mr. Chow.

He was hilarious, razor-sharp and clearly feeling the glow of becoming one of the industry's next big things. I am always happy when, after doing this for so many years, a talent can get me feeling like anything is possible.

"I love *Nip/Tuck*," I told him. "In particular I love love love the character of Dr. Christian Troy. It's such a great part. Funny, sexy, cocky but also clearly broken inside. I love how complicated you've written him, the bravado barely covering the self-loathing. It's the best leading-man part on television."

Ryan cocked his head and gave me a look that clearly said, "Are you *crazy*?" A little thrown, I rattled on.

"Seriously, the dialogue you give him! My wife and I were watching last week and I told her, 'Now *that's* the kind of role I should do! Where is my version of Dr. Christian Troy?!'"

Ryan went pale. I wondered if he'd had a bad piece of fish. He was staring at me like I was an alien.

"Um, Rob, you *do* know that I wrote Christian Troy for you, right?" he asked.

"Wh-what?!"

"I wrote the part for you. I had your picture on my computer while I did it. It's no surprise to me that it spoke to you. I designed it for you."

I was stunned. How could this be? One of the few brilliantly written leading-man parts around and I never knew about it, read it or knew that it was written for me?

We finally figured out what had happened, and it is vintage television business 101. Comparing notes, we learned that Ryan had turned the script in to our mutual agents and told them he wanted me. My agents (doing their job) were on the lookout for only the best and biggest next step after *The West Wing*. And pre-*Nip/Tuck* Ryan was just one of many midlevel guys hoping to get a shot with their own show.

"I suppose there's no way your agents would let you work for a tiny cable network and its low budget coming off a monster like *The West Wing*," he said, and I knew he was right.

"But you'd think they'd at least give me the script!" I said, even though I knew this kind of thing happened every day.

"Yes, but you're forgetting one thing," he replied. "I wasn't Ryan Murphy yet!"

Why is it that we always think the unpleasant things that happen to so many will never happen to us but expect the good things that happen to so few will *absolutely* happen for us?

It's not like I didn't have experience with this phenomenon. Yet

I still thought the politics of show business would never ding me. Conversely, I also thought that if I were in the same position as others upon whom fortune smiled I would be rewarded in kind.

I remember one day on *The West Wing*, standing with my pal the late John Spencer, who played Leo. The previous week, the show had won a then-unprecedented number of Emmys in its first season and was exploding in the zeitgeist. The entire cast and crew had been summoned together for "an announcement and presentation" by the corporate brass. It was unheard-of to shut down shooting for such a thing, and with our Emmys and cultural domination in full flower, both John and I assumed we were in for something special.

As we crammed into the Roosevelt Room set waiting for the executives to arrive, everyone buzzed about what this "presentation" would be. Recently Paramount had given Tom Cruise a Porsche for some movie that performed well for them. The "Friends" were all being paid crazy money, and the cast of *Will and Grace* (on our same network) had all been given matching black Porsches. Our *West Wing* producer John Wells had famously given a number of actors and some of the crew on *ER*, which he also produced, each a check for a million dollars. Even midlevel shows were rewarding successes. Just that month, the star of another NBC show called *Providence*, Melina Kanakaredes, had been presented with a brand-new Range Rover. It was an era of show-business excess and was completely outrageous, but if it was happening to shows much less successful than *The West Wing*, both John and I thought, why not us!

After waiting for quite a while, eating up valuable shooting time, the actors, producers and crew were getting antsy. Mercifully, I overheard a mysterious young man in a suit and a Secret Service–type headset say, "Traveling! They are traveling!" as a fleet of junior executives made ready for the honchos' imminent arrival.

"Whaddaya think we're getting?" said John with that beautiful, mirthful twinkle that I miss so much. "Ya think it's a car? I heard the 'Friends' all got cars!"

"How cool would *that* be!" I replied.

We looked at each other and giggled both in excitement and at the absurdity of it all.

Then a hush fell over the room as the top executive made his entrance.

"Thank you all so much for taking time off from shooting today. You, the cast and crew of *The West Wing*, last week won more Emmys than any television show in its first season in history. This show is the best example in our long corporate history of who we are as a company. Your excellence, your intelligence, your humor and your wide and growing audience make all of us, and our shareholders, unspeakably proud. We only thought it fitting that we present you with a token of our gratitude and a physical acknowledgment of each of your exemplary work."

Proudly, he gestured to an aide, who stepped outside and returned wheeling what looked to be a room service cart with a sheet over it.

"I don't think it's a car," said John under his breath.

"So, from all of us, to all of you . . . Congratulations, *West Wing!*" said the boss as he whipped the sheet off with a flourish. "Enjoy!"

Sitting on the tray was a single-serving espresso maker.

At first we all thought it was a gag. It wasn't. The room stared in disbelief. The brass filed out as if they had delivered gold bullion.

"Do . . . do we all get one of those?" a crew member said finally.

"No, this is for everyone, we will place it on the food table where everyone can enjoy it!" said the Secret Service suit.

And that's exactly what happened until a week later, when it broke. When we looked to return it we discovered it was rented.

The truth is there is no perfect industry. There are great people and great opportunities for all of us in whatever line we are in. Also, I love the entertainment business. In many ways, it's all I've ever known, and originally, it was all I ever wanted. The trick is to keep looking forward. You have a hit, you move on, you have a flop, you move on even faster.

One day I received a phone call from Les Moonves, the president of CBS. Les is the king of network presidents. There is no one more successful and I'd always hoped to be in business with him.

"Rob, those guys at NBC should *never* have pulled *Lyon's Den*. It was really good and getting better *and* they should have been thrilled with those numbers," he told me.

"Thanks, Les, that means a lot coming from you," I said, and it was true.

"Anyway, I'm sending you a show we'd love you to star in. It could be great and we'd love to have you in the CBS family."

I was flattered; CBS, under Les, was the biggest network around. His dramas, like the *CSI* franchises, *NCIS* and *Without a Trace*, were huge moneymakers and huge hits. Maybe this was the opportunity I had been looking for.

The show in question was called *Dr. Vegas*. In spite of the fact that I hated the title and with Les's words ringing in my ears, I told my agents and managers I was interested. Although it wasn't "on the page," as they say, buried within the concept I saw an opportunity to make something much more edgy and raw. The setup was this: I would play an in-house Vegas casino doctor. He'd work for a larger-than-life casino mogul and battle a bad gambling habit. On any given week he would tend to a litany of interesting characters that inhabited the flashy/glitzy/high-stakes/sad/desperate and wild world that is modern Las Vegas. As I write this now, that still sounds like a promising world for storytelling!

I wanted to steer the tone away from the cheesy, old-school Vegas tropes. No showgirls and mob guys. I hoped to do stories about kids on ecstasy and the (then-new) explosion of cool nightclubs and big-name promoters. Sure, we would do traditional stories about boxers and ringside medical high jinks, but I also wanted to explore the *real* Vegas of average folk who live totally outside the neon, who get paid to work in the bedlam of the Strip but never actually go out there themselves. Or, if we were to do a story about a call girl, instead of setting it in some hotel penthouse, make it about her daily life living in a condo way off the Strip. I wanted a Vegas we hadn't seen before. I wanted it to be *real*.

I wanted to do to the genre what *Nip/Tuck* did to doctors. Probably still smarting from that missed opportunity, I wanted to make this my *Nip/Tuck* on the Strip, with all of its black humor and edge protruding through the sex, fun and glamour.

After a week of negotiating, my deal was done, although not yet signed. It was then that I got an urgent phone call from the producers of a potential new show for ABC called *Grey's Anatomy*.

In spite of having a deal in principle on *Dr. Vegas*, I agreed to meet the people making *Grey's Anatomy*. I had read it and loved it—the writing was crisp, real and very entertaining—and it's always a good idea to hear out talented people.

"We would be thrilled if you would play Dr. Derek Shepherd," they said right off the bat.

I told them about my negotiations on *Dr. Vegas*. "I'm pretty far down the line with them," I said.

"But you'd be *so* great in this!" they said.

It was a fantastic role, and I could easily see myself doing it and having a blast. I was positive and enthusiastic with them but noncommittal.

I was torn. *Grey's* was a much better script; in fact there was no comparison. But *Dr. Vegas* had potential to become something more original than a hospital soap. I asked my manager how ABC felt about the show and my joining it. The network never responded. On the other hand, at CBS the attention was relentless.

"I understand they want you for some show on ABC," Les said the next day. "Let me tell you how it is. ABC is the lowest-rated network on television. They haven't had a new hit in years. They haven't launched a successful new *drama* in *eleven seasons*! What makes you think this show will be any different?" They were all true and important points.

"At CBS we have *all* the top dramas and have new ones that break out every year. We make hits and we know how to sell them once we do. You deserve to be with us."

Les was too much of a gentleman to mention that we also had a deal in spirit, although it would hardly have been the first time one went south at the eleventh hour: "Let's make a show!" he said.

In life you have to put yourself in the best position to win. A great playbook means nothing if you don't have the right people to execute it. Also, I've always subscribed to the theory that the definition of insanity is doing the same thing over and over again while expecting different results. Year after year after year, all of ABC's new dramas flopped. CBS was on a hot streak that continues to this day. Although *Grey's Anatomy* was a far better script, I chose *Dr. Vegas*. The odds were just too stacked.

Unfortunately, I had just eaten what my pal Mike Myers would call a "wish sandwich." Which is to say that in lieu of something tangible (and edible) I instead chose a "vision," a "promise" of what could and should be, "potential" and "hope," something I "wished" to transform into something better, and swallowed it whole. I hadn't yet learned that even if you are lucky enough to have collaborators who are creatively on the same page, it is extraordinarily difficult to take the seeds of an idea in a script and grow them into trees. And it's almost impossible to convince anyone to cut down the big themes they've already written to make room for your saplings. But I thought I could. I "wished" I could. I was convinced I could take what I saw in my head and make it real. Time would tell.

The first order of business was casting.

More than anything else, I wanted to bring edge and real dramatic stakes to the show. I wanted to get rid of the "soft" elements, of which there were many. I hoped to accomplish this two ways: by staying away from story lines that had no real, believable jeopardy for the show's characters and by casting actors who had true depth. For the costarring part of the casino owner, I wanted the not-yet-commonly-known-as-bat-shit-crazy Tom Sizemore.

This was before his numerous drug busts and scrapes with the law, before the reality TV show and fourth, fifth and sixth chances. He was still "Sarge" from *Saving Private Ryan*. He was the stud actor from Michael Mann's *Heat*. He was the new Gene Hackman, but with sexual danger. He was the *exact* flavor I was looking for as a template for the show's tone. A dangerous, great actor with charisma.

No one liked the idea. In fairness, Tom had just had a failed show on CBS and there were rumors of misbehavior. There was a push for Joey Pantoliano, whom I loved in *The Sopranos*.

It doesn't matter if you're a lawyer, a soldier, a dude at a bar trying to close with a girl or an actor producing a TV show: You've got to know when to fold your hand. Keeping your capital and living to fight the battles you might actually win is critical.

"I'd love to work with Joey," I said. I knew he could go as dark as I wanted and, unlike Tom, could handle a joke if needed. Also, I knew he was one of the great pros in the business.

Joey was cast.

For the part of my nurse and will-they-or-won't-they love interest, we all agreed on Amy Adams after seeing her in *Catch Me If You Can*. Clearly, she was a substantive actress, beautiful but not in a TV way and very, very smart. And together, she and I had the one thing you can't fake: chemistry.

The last remaining lead role was the casino host, a character who would be the "fixer" for any of the hotel's issues.

"What about Sizemore for *that*?" I asked. "C'mon, guys. He's one of the greatest character actors of our generation!" I said, pushing.

No one disagreed, but still they thought Tom was a huge liability. Maybe being fourteen years sober at the time had something to do with my confidence that I could be a positive influence if needed.

"I will be all over him. I will keep him together," I said. I also believe in redemption and the importance of second chances. And I *hate* whisper campaigns about any actor's being "difficult." In my experience it's usually the other way around. The "troublesome" performer is often just doing whatever it takes to protect their work or the project in the face of nincompoops and others who don't give a shit. It's the actor's face on the screen, after all.

Begrudgingly, an offer was made to Tom Sizemore. When they couldn't come to terms, I paid for the difference out of my own salary. Finally Tom was in.

Soon, I would learn the veracity of the clichés "Be careful what you wish for" *and* "No good deed goes unpunished."

One day, in the production office, I noticed a stream of stunning, leggy blondes filing in and out of the casting department.

I discovered, to my horror, that without informing me, there had been a mandate to "sex up" the cast. A new character, a hot, blond waitress, had been created to fill the quota.

I was upset. I was the lead actor, I was a producer and at some point, clearly, I would be playing footsie with this new hottie. How could an entire story line and character have been created without my being in the loop?

I had to stand up for myself and the vision of the show I *thought* we'd all agreed on. "I have Amy Adams as a love interest already!" I pointed out.

"Amy Adams is not sexy enough to be the love interest," I was told.

What makes an actor a star is among the more subjective concepts one can debate. I believed that Amy was not only a star but perfectly capable of being anyone's love interest. But there was no way to prove it. So, again, I backed down, knowing I couldn't win and not wanting to be a lone dissenting voice. At that point in my career, I was still operating under the theory that if you gave in to "the powers that be," down the road you would in return have some goodwill to use as collateral.

And so our cast had a surprise late addition. Sarah Lancaster, a beautiful and kind twentysomething, became the show's last lead part.

We began shooting *Dr. Vegas* at two A.M. in the casino of the Green Valley Inn. We would start at that time every day and finish at two P.M., maybe the worst hours imaginable. You couldn't sleep, couldn't eat. But it was the only way to use their casino.

After the first week the director was fired. When we got to our second episode a new head writer was brought in. Again, the early warning signs were everywhere. But I was glad that my bosses were on top of it and willing to make changes to improve the show. There was no laissez-faire self-delusion this time.

As with *The Lyon's Den*, I really enjoyed the crew and our great cast. Joey Pantoliano, or "Joey Pants," as he is known to everyone, is one of the great characters in Hollywood. From *The Matrix* to *The Fugitive* to *The Sopranos*, he's got great chops and anyone you ask loves him.

Recently, Joey had taken to using an earpiece when acting, à la Marlon Brando. He implanted a tiny transmitter into his left ear, into which his lines were read by an assistant sitting offstage. A hidden microphone in his costume relayed the dialogue spoken to him to the assistant so she knew when to prompt Joey. Sometimes I would forget he had this contraption on.

ME: Hey, Joey, how was your weekend?
JOEY: Good, man. Took it easy, rested. My wife and I caught up. What did you do this—

(Suddenly into his chest)

No, three P.M. doesn't work for me. What? . . . No . . . I said three P.M. That's right . . . okay . . . let me know.

(back to me)

Sorry, anyway, what did you do this weekend?

If you didn't know that he was wearing an earpiece and talking to his hidden assistant, you might think he had Tourette's syndrome. But Joey was a team player, always working to be his best, never phoning it in and always bringing his wonderful mix of humor and danger. He was a great arm to lean on, especially when the shit hit the fan once again, this time over Amy Adams.

Someone at the studio or the network (I didn't know who; you never know the "who" involved when it's a bad decision like this) wanted to drop Amy from the show. A number of reasons were given, but try as I might I could never get a straight read. Her full option to appear in all episodes of *Dr. Vegas* was not picked up. A compromise was made and I got to hold on to her for as long as I could negotiate, which was six episodes. Obviously I was wildly unhappy and Amy wasn't thrilled either about being out of a job.

I once was told that in the days of the Bible, wildfires and burning shrubs were fairly common. Back then you might see a burning bush on your daily morning commute into town. So when Moses saw the burning bush, what was significant was that he stopped and realized that this one was different. *This* burning bush was special. This one was a sign.

I try to hold on to the things I believe to be good and true. Good things happen to good people. Karma is real. There is a larger, better plan for us all if we stay positive, keep pushing and get out of our own way. But life can beat you down. Life loves to test your belief in the unprovable, your unsubstantiated faith in a larger goodwill. Sometimes it even feels like the more you believe, the more you are tested. And that's when it's very important not to mistake a burning bush for a random shrub fire.

With Amy's sad departure from the show, I lost a very special actor and she lost a job. But for her, it would be a gift, and for me, it would be a sign. Amy had planned on starring with me on a hopefully big CBS drama and suddenly, that was over. So she was able to have a meeting on a movie she would have been otherwise unavailable for. The movie was *Junebug,* and she got the part. The role earned her an Academy Award nomination. It launched her into the A-list. The *Dr. Vegas* disaster was her gift. Sometimes you have to get fired to get hired.

On the days when I still doubt my love for the business, when I am sick of the double-speak and the dumbing down, when I tire of being judged project to project, when the realities that everyone faces in any line of work get me down, I remember that I was sent a sign. It wasn't just another actor being replaced, it was a message: The "best" plans unbuckle in an instant. Prepare to be disappointed and left without viable options. But also be prepared for this to be the greatest event that has ever happened to you. Like it was for Amy Adams. Like I believe it can be for all of us.

———

The day after *Dr. Vegas* premiered, I crawled out of my bed in the back of my Suburban to the sight of Joey Pants packing up his trailer.

"Saw our numbers last night. This one ain't long for the world, pal," he said, carrying a box of knickknacks to his car.

Joey was an alarmist and always dramatic. I do not allow myself the luxury of defeatism. "C'mon, man. We can turn it around!" I said, heading into another pre-sunrise rehearsal.

Hour-long shows have a rating at the first half hour and one in the second. When the first rating is good, it means they like the stars and the idea of the show. If the rating goes down in the second half hour it means they don't like the episode itself. Usually it means the story didn't hook them, so they bailed. It's pretty simple and it's a very clear message.

With the notable exceptions of *The West Wing* and *Parks and Recreation*, I almost never read an episode of TV and don't think "This needs to be better." But few shows have the level of writing that those shows have. It's obvious and it's right there on the page for all to see.

On *Dr. Vegas* our second-half ratings bore out my suspicions: Our stories were soft and needed teeth to hold the viewers.

Tom Sizemore had been doing great work on camera. Brooding, dark, sometimes funny but with a threat of real violence underneath. But the writing consistently steered away from anything even close to dark, even with the new replacement head writer. *Dr. Vegas*'s tone was cutesy, faux-sexy, without any real tension and absolutely zero danger. It could not have been further away from a network version of *Nip/Tuck*. But I kept trying to drag it just a little closer.

I pitched a story line that I hoped would show the network that we could push the envelope. In the story line, Tom Sizemore's character would kill a man with his bare hands. It would be retribution for the murder-robbery the man committed in our casino. As Tom killed the criminal, you would feel guilt about feeling so good about Tom as a vigilante. These morally ambivalent stories are today common on cable drama. But on big, highly viewed networks, particularly CBS, this would be very, very dark indeed. Showing very good faith, the studio and network let us give it a try. You can't ask for more from your bosses.

After giving up some of my salary to close Sizemore's deal, I also got him with my business manager. I kept a protective eye out in all areas I could. I didn't pry into things that weren't my business and hoped that my proximity would be a steadying influence if the time came.

The time came.

I had noticed Tom sweating unseasonably, noticed he was wearing mirrored sunglasses almost nonstop, noticed dilated eyes and a change in personality. Tom was, and is, capable of being very charming and always liked to tell stories, usually about Robert De Niro. There wasn't a conversation that Tom couldn't work "Bobby" De Niro into.

"Bobby got me this shirt."

"Bobby wanted to adopt me," etc.

I love eccentric actors and their stories, but when Tom told me that he played walk-on football at Notre Dame for a single play, I knew something was awry. And despite his increasing tardiness to the set (never a good sign), he was always great in his scenes. Even if he sweated through an entire wardrobe before lunch to do it.

But as luck would have it, when I finally got the dark, intense script I'd been pushing for, with Tom at the center, he lost it. And lost it big-time.

My cell phone went off in the middle of the night. It was Tom. He was crying, screaming and wailing in a way that sounded inhuman. He hadn't said a word and already I was scared.

"AAAAAARGGH! AAAAAARRRRRHH!" he shrieked.

"Tom! Tom! What's going on?"

"Whaaaaaah! Grrraaaah!"

"Tom! Stop it! What's happening?! Are you okay?!" I yelled into the phone.

"My— My— My girlfriend's dead! AAAAWWWGH! Oh God, she's deaaaaad!!" he sobbed.

"What!! Jesus Christ, Tom, what?!" I said, trying to get a grip on what was happening.

"They— They— They cut off her head! AAAAAARRRGGH! Oh God, it's inside of a Dumpster! Waaaaaah!"

"Wait a minute, Tom. Stop. Slow down."

"They hacked. They hacked. They hacked up my poor girlfriend! They took her head. It's in a Dumpster. The downtown Dumpster!! AAAGGNNPH!!"

It went on like this for minutes before he got around to telling me what the call was *really* about.

"And— And— And— I can't come in to shoot today 'cause I'm looking for her torso! Aagh, Rob, she has no torso!!"

There was more screaming and then the line went dead.

My wife rolled over and looked at the clock, which read three forty-five A.M.

"Who was that, honey?"

"Oh, it was Tom Sizemore calling to say he won't be coming to work."

That morning, when he was indeed a no-show, we were forced to shoot without him. After a long day of scrambling to shoot out of order, I tracked Tom down, threw him in my Suburban and drove him to a drug rehab. I didn't know what the fallout would be, but Tom needed help, and fast. Whatever would happen next would happen tomorrow, after all. One day at a time.

We shot the script I had such high hopes for anyway. We promoted a very inexperienced actor to handle Tom's part, which was reduced so dramatically that it had none of the dark power we had intended. The episode was a mess. The chance to change the course of the show was lost.

The powers that be were supportive and gracious. Tom kept his job even though he would be in a thirty-day rehab. But his workload was reduced to almost nothing, throwing the writing staff for a loop from which we never recovered. Now, with both Amy Adams and effectively Tom Sizemore gone, there were two times fewer storytelling opportunities, not to mention two fewer irreplaceable actors.

Dr. Vegas could not be revived and it died on the table. Found in its system at the time of death were good people with good intentions, a lack of a common creative point of view, bland writing, inconsistent acting and an element of cheese that was simply too strong to kill with conventional medicine.

Tom Sizemore would bounce in and out of rehab. I would visit and listen as he told his wild stories, wearing a do-rag, hiding behind those mirrored aviators. Ultimately, he was a man who simply could not or would not get honest with himself. Folks who can't almost never get sober. But I pray his day will come. And I will be there for him when it does.

Maybe I'm in denial, but I don't believe in "flops." You try something and it may not work. You try something and this time it might. You never know, and you have no choice other than to keep trying. The only time you flop is when you don't learn something.

I don't eat wish sandwiches anymore. Today, when I read a script, I assume it will *never* get better, that there will be no changes to anything on the page. Just like how I try to judge people by what they actually say and do and not by what I know they have the *potential* to do.

There are signs and gifts everywhere, particularly in setbacks, but you need to keep your eyes peeled. They come wrapped in missed opportunities, in unfulfilled promises and lost jobs. They come born out of disappointments you never saw coming and also in those you should have. But they bring you better things and take you to where you were *meant* to go. Like my son Johnowen in Little League, you've gotta run hard on the base paths. All roads lead to Rome. Our setbacks bring us forward; we wander in the wilderness so the road can bring us home.

MARLINS

MVP
Sports Cards

JOHNOWEN
LOWE

SHORTSTOP   2000

My MVP, Johnowen.

Freedom and Love

When my brother Chad and I would visit our grandparents, which we did often and for long periods of time, we would sometimes talk our grandpa into the drive-in or "a show," as he called movies, at Sidney, Ohio's gorgeous 1920s-era movie palace. He would only attend movies that had "a moral." In the early seventies, although that era is now considered the last golden age of movies, Grandpa hadn't been to a movie, unless shanghaied by his grandkids, since *Dr. Zhivago*.

My grandfather was the kind of man I didn't totally understand in my youth. Born dirt-poor in a family of eight in rural Ohio, he dropped out of school and set out on his own when the family couldn't feed him. He was in the eighth grade. He would become a butcher, a grocer and eventually the owner of the Spot restaurant for almost fifty years. It stands to this day, serving the best hamburger and old-fashioned cream pie you will find under one roof. Despite his lack of education, Grandpa was a leader of the business community and the first person in Shelby County to drive a Cadillac, which he replaced every year. He was a Nixon supporter with no time for hippies, a churchgoing Methodist and a scratch golfer with seven holes in one to his credit. He loved fishing and cigars and let me sit on his lap while he smoked them, even as we drove in the fast lane of I–75. He traveled to every World Series with a group of guys and, like so many in the seventies, started a jogging club that met every Sunday before church, until most of the members dropped dead from heart attacks anyway. He was also married to the same woman for fifty years. His tough, unyielding will and commitment were hard to get my arms around as a young boy but unendingly inspirational to me as a young man.

Upon his death in 1991 I discovered among his belongings an award from Rotary for perfect attendance over *five decades*. Newly sober at the time, I could barely get it together to get to a few AA meetings with consistency, even when I knew they were saving my life! But Grandpa's half a century of commitment to business and his wife became a road map for me moving forward as I rebuilt my life from the ground up. I don't know if I will be able to live with his level of integrity and consistency, but I know I'm lucky to have been left with his example. I also know that getting to fifty years of anything is actually more simple than it sounds: You do it one day at a time.

My grandfather was also unapologetically patriotic. When I was a boy, I never understood his flag on the lapel, given that the whole country was watching our president go down in deserved flames courtesy of the Watergate hearings. Additionally, my parents and certainly everyone of their generation were virulently anti–Vietnam War and therefore antigovernment by proxy. My grandpa seemed to me to be holding on to some vision of America that was being debunked nightly on the news, and it made me wonder what he saw that I didn't.

Ironically, as I grew into a man and began to see our world through my own eyes and experience, I began to drift toward a love of country that I first recognized in him. In Hollywood, where everyone's respect for the president is contingent on what party he comes from, I found myself, like my grandpa, swimming against the tide of popular sentiment. Well before I did a show about it, I was convinced of the inherent goodness of the majority of the men and women who served our country, Republican or Democrat. I read memoirs by ex-presidents, followed the ebb and flow of their administrations. As it did with Grandpa, something about the history of America spoke to me on a very deep level. And I never knew why. Until recently.

I was always envious of families who were well steeped in ancestral lore. Mine wasn't. We had no stories of relatives long gone who did great or even interesting things. But I was curious about our family's past, so when a television documentary series offered to put a team of genealogists on the case, I said yes.

For a year and a half they followed every strand of my family and dug and researched wherever it led them. If, at the end, they found nothing interesting or entertaining, they would move on to another public figure who might have more compelling forefathers.

They looked at every branch of my father's line first. Then they turned to my mother's. At some point they began following her father, my grandpa. That led them to John Christopher East—my great-great-great-great-great-grandfather. The closest connection I had to him was my grandpa's mother, the ancient and puppet-show-loving Bessie Mae East, in her walk-up apartment, where she would put a kerchief on her hand and perform plays for me. John Christopher, it turned out, started her line in this country, which then flowed through Bessie to Grandpa, to my mother and then to me.

As I learned his story I began to understand both my grandfather and myself through the events of his life. Events I never could have imagined that explain so much about how I feel about so many things.

John Christopher East was born in 1754 in tiny Fürstenhagen, Germany. Filming the documentary, I stood in the chapel where he was baptized and read the original church records of my family's births, marriages and deaths from the late 1500s. Remarkably, I was able to visit the house where he was born, with tile and Formica covering its six-hundred-year-old beams.

Fürstenhagen lies in the region called Hesse-Kassel, a former principality of the many German states that existed until their unification. For almost a hundred years before Christopher East's birth, it was mandatory that all able-bodied young men leave their mothers, girlfriends, wives and all they'd ever known to be conscripted, often against their will, to fight as paid soldiers throughout the world. The boys from Hesse-Kassel were state of the art, infamous and feared in spite of the fact that many of them had no will or desire to fight in the first place. Named for the area they hailed from, they became known as Hessians.

Even today, the phrase "Hessian soldier" brings to mind images of large, powerful, resplendently uniformed, cold-blooded mercenary killers. One of the most frightening characters in American literature is a Hessian soldier, the Headless Horseman in "The Legend of Sleepy Hollow." But the reality was that many a teenage boy was press-ganged into service or killed on the spot if he dared to desert. While the families at home did receive a decent payment for the services of their sons, it was the state, led by Landgrave Frederick the Second, that reaped the lion's share of cash paid out from foreign armies looking to bring in the best of the best. So much for the "Age of Enlightenment."

In the early spring of 1776, East joined the other boys of his village (forgive me if I call them "boys"; Christopher Eastor Oeste, as he was called in German, would've been around the same age as my son Matthew . . .) on a march that would eventually lead them through the thawing countryside to a flotilla of awaiting boats. They were told they were traveling across the great ocean to America, where they would help defend the colonists against savage Indians. Obviously, the reality would be very different.

One of Christopher East's shipmates, nineteen-year-old Johannes Reuber, kept a detailed journal that survives to this day. I read from it at the Library of Congress in Washington, DC. It tells a vivid tale of a voyage gone badly. A crossing that should have taken weeks instead took almost four months, as their ship languished in the middle of the Atlantic waiting for wind. Like all kids everywhere, the boys would ask their superiors, "Are we there yet?" The Hessian high command would answer by laughing in their faces. These officers were men of business and ran the boat accordingly. When their youngest conscript, a fifteen-year-old who was the ship's mascot, was washed overboard, there was no thought of stopping to save him. The diary contains a harrowing scene of the crowded deck as they all watched the pleading boy flail as the ship sailed onward.

The Hessians finally arrived at Staten Island, in New York Harbor, just weeks after the signing of the Declaration of Independence. Christopher was made a "grenadier," which meant he was part of the elite hand-to-hand fighters—the biggest, strongest and most notoriously courageous, who would be the first to storm the battlefield. He was placed under the command of General von Rall, one of the most decorated and experienced military minds in the field. They, along with all the other Hessians, would join the British forces under the supreme command of General William Howe. My ancestor had arrived in America at the beginning of its revolution and he wouldn't be fighting Indians; on August 27, 1776, Christopher instead went to battle against General George Washington.

The Battle of Long Island was a rout. Washington was defeated and after vicious, up-close, hand-to-hand fighting with Christopher's grenadiers, his army ran for their lives. Within days, George Washington and the Continental Army had lost New York City.

The lauded Hessians, buttressing their British paymasters, now prepared to crush the revolution in its infancy by marching directly on Philadelphia. After securing New York and its harbor, the British and Hessian forces, along with Christopher East, set up winter camp in Trenton, New Jersey.

There are moments in time, battles in war, that change the fabric of the world. The Battle of Trenton was one. Christopher East would've been asleep, possibly hungover after a Christmas celebration, on December 27, 1776, when, in a Hail Mary to save America, George Washington crossed the Delaware in a sneak attack, changing the course of the war, our fledgling nation and therefore the future of the world.

As the surprised British Army and its Hessian support tried to rally in the sleeting, frigid dawn, they were caught in a brutal, violent but short battle. Christopher, on that day, fought for his life face-to-face and elbow-to-elbow with destiny's chosen.

Present and fighting with the father of our country that cold morning were some of the greatest leaders America would ever know. In the blood and the gore of a street-scene battlefield that wasn't very big at all, Christopher faced down two additional future presidents of the United States, James Madison and James Monroe; the future chief justice of the Supreme Court responsible for most of today's constitutional law and for making the court a separate and coequal branch of government, John Marshall; and future legendary statesmen (and later mortal enemies) Alexander Hamilton and Aaron Burr.

Christopher East was taken as a prisoner. In all likelihood, he was marched past his dying commander, von Rall, whose last words to George Washington were "Look after my men," as was noted by Washington in his diary. About von Rall and his Hessian sons Washington marveled that rarely, if ever, had he seen such dignified bravery.

I went to Trenton and then to the neighboring church where Christopher and a thousand of his fellows were held prisoner before the long march to Philadelphia, whose citizens lined the streets, hitting and spitting in the faces of the defeated prisoners.

In the old church graveyard I noticed beautiful, small markers planted before a small number of weathered headstones.

"What do those markers signify?" I asked.

"They mark the graves of revolutionary patriots. They are markers of the Sons and Daughters of the American Revolution."

"I see," I said, and my eyes misted. A crew was filming me and I became embarrassed by my emotion, so I turned away from the graves. A production assistant arrived with news that he had discovered a nearby Starbucks. Later, in the bustle of today's America, I sipped my double-espresso macchiato and thought of the men back in the ground, behind the church.

I wished Christopher had been among them. I wished he had fought with and maybe known these heroes, these early men of our country. But his destiny had placed him on the other side.

But there was more to the story.

One day, I received a package from one of the lead researchers on my family's history recounting new details about Christopher's life after being taken prisoner by George Washington's men. After being marched through Philadelphia, Christopher was kept in the notoriously horrendous and intimidating prison at Lancaster, Pennsylvania, which stands today.

Like all Hessian prisoners of war, he was eventually offered amnesty in exchange for deserting the British Army. He took the offer and faded into the Pennsylvania farmlands. He was one of the few who chose not to return home at the war's end. Of the thirty thousand Hessians who came to fight, only five thousand stayed. Why was Christopher among those few?

The researcher's package contained a photocopy of some kind of ledger from 1782 and a letter addressed to me. I examined the ledger first. Although it was faded, you could clearly see the original handwriting. It appeared to be a small list of early settlers of Donegal Township, Pennsylvania, and a ledger of taxes paid. Christopher's name was there, along with his payment.

I turned next to the letter. It was from the Sons of the American Revolution. It explained that the document was a record of a Revolutionary War effort supply tax to which Christopher had contributed, "serving the cause for Freedom." As a result of walking away from the British army, choosing freedom and then contributing to its cause financially, John Christopher East was now officially a patriot of the revolution. He had come full circle, from forced combatant to actively working for the American cause. The letter went on to welcome me as a new member of the Sons of the American Revolution.

The people I admire the most are those who have the courage, foresight and ability to see themselves with cold-eyed honesty and fundamentally change themselves. Those who, with no guarantees of greater success or happiness, find it in themselves to completely alter the course of their lives to follow what is oftentimes just a small voice telling them that they can do better. That they can *be* better.

Perhaps John Christopher East perceived the greatness around him at Trenton and later throughout the new America. It must have changed him fundamentally. He gave up all he had ever known to stay in a foreign land instead of returning home. He had arrived here and been told to kill. But in the end, he fell in love. With a young country and its promise of personal freedom and, later, with a young woman named Maria and the promise of family. And like most who take the risk to follow love, the promises were rewarded. I wouldn't be here otherwise.

I believe we're all influenced by our epigenetic legacies. From the time I was small, I was interested in government. When my grade-school pals played kickball, I sold Kool-Aid for George McGovern. I followed the minutiae of the White House long before I worked there playing Sam Seaborn in *The West Wing*. When Sheryl and I built our home its elevation was inspired by Mount Vernon, although I had never seen it in person. For years before knowing this surprising story, hanging above our fireplace was an original oil portrait of . . . George Washington. Learning my family's history filled in the gaps of why I had always been drawn to those things.

But in spite of my early interest in politics, I had to learn to better love my country. My grandfather's support of the Vietnam War, Nixon and the events at Kent State were a barrier to seeing America in its true totality. The worldview of my youth had to be reshaped by time, experience and travel. Like my ancestor, I was better able to see my home after crossing an ocean and spending time in foreign lands. What he saw and learned made him never return to his home. What I learned made me never want to leave mine.

I am the son of my grandfathers. I sometimes imagine I can feel them in my blood guiding me. And even though it's just a historical organization membership and some may think it's silly, I'm proud to be a Son of the American Revolution. It inspires me to try to make the same choices for the same reasons that John Christopher did. For freedom and for love.

My Grandpa and I in 1976.

On the banks of the Delaware, which George Washington crossed in 1776 to confront my (5x) Great Grandfather.

An Actor Prepares

One of my favorite parts of being an actor is the preparation that goes into creating a character. There is no right way or wrong way. For the most part, every actor does it differently, although there are some universally accepted secret tricks of the trade.

After our run together on *The West Wing*, Aaron Sorkin and I took his first brilliant calling card, the play *A Few Good Men*, to London's West End, for its revival. I loved the movie but was really fascinated with the play it was based on, which Sorkin famously wrote on cocktail napkins while working as an usher at the Palace Theatre on Broadway. I remembered the commotion it caused when it opened with a post-*Amadeus* Tom Hulce in the starring role of LTJG Kaffee. Only a few other guys played the role onstage and I knew them all: Timothy Busfield, Bradley Whitford and Michael O'Keefe. They always talked about the power of the part, how, in front of a live audience, it was the kind of role that is the rarest of all, huge and demanding, onstage basically curtain to curtain, extremely dialogue-heavy, romantic, passionate and very funny (I didn't see a ton of humor in the film version, so I was always curious about that). Aaron felt Kaffee was tailor-made for me. The London revival of A Few Good Men was booked into the West End's most storied theater, the Royal Haymarket, home to Oscar Wilde and John Gielgud.

Obviously, I wanted to try my hand.

Although my first role onstage was at nine years old, I hadn't been onstage in a decade. In the early nineties I had done a run on Broadway in a Feydeau farce, but it was an ensemble. In London, this part was the lead and the show would succeed or fail on the shoulders of its hero, the cocky naval lawyer.

I was worried about my voice. Sorkin's characters are notably verbose and the show was packed with monologues made famous by the movie version. I knew that every night, people would be waiting for "You can't handle the truth!" I wanted to make sure that by show one hundred, I could still deliver. I also didn't want to ever miss a show. Having never carried a play of this scope and pedigree, there was no guarantee. I needed to go into training. Luckily, I knew who to call: an expert I'd met years ago for a very big potential project.

In 1991, during a matinee of my Broadway show, the stage manager told me that I had a call on the backstage phone.

"He says it's Sir Andrew Lloyd Webber!" he said, eyes popping out of his head.

Andrew Lloyd Webber's calling midperformance on a pay phone in the middle of a Feydeau farce on Broadway should have seemed like a prank, but somehow I knew it was real even before I heard his voice.

"Hello, Rob, sorry to bother you but I've seen the show and I want to work with you."

I was hugely flattered. Being welcomed by the gatekeepers of areas that I'm not established in is always a goal of mine. I need to expand and try new things. Andrew Lloyd Webber wanted to help.

"Have you heard of my show *Joseph and the Amazing Technicolor Dreamcoat?*"

Who hadn't? I passed its giant billboard in Times Square on the way to the theater every day.

"I want you as Joseph for its London run." I was honored but hesitant. Did Mr. Lloyd Webber know whether I could sing? Did he even care? Maybe he was the one person out of the billion watching who liked my duet with Snow White at the Oscars.

"Wow! I don't know what to say!" I said truthfully. It was a big vote of confidence from the master of the musical.

But I knew it wasn't the right fit for me. As much as I like to stretch and take chances, I also didn't want to be shirtless, holding that gaudy dreamcoat four stories high on billboards everywhere. *Joseph* had always struck me as a little cheesy. I had another idea.

"I hear you are making a musical of my favorite movie," I said.

"What movie is that?"

"*Sunset Boulevard.*"

"I am!" he said. "We are doing an investors' showcase at Sidmonton"—his estate—"soon."

"Well *that* would be something I'd love to do," I said. I had always thought Joe, played by William Holden, was one of the great parts in film history. If anyone could make it as good in a musical, it was Webber. It could be one for the ages.

The second act was beginning so we agreed to talk further. Later, after a few more attempts to put me in the coat of many colors, he finally offered me the part I wanted in *Sunset Boulevard*. But in the end, the dates conflicted with a version of Tennessee Williams's *Suddenly, Last Summer* I was doing with Richard Eyre and Maggie Smith. And as everyone today knows, you never renege on the dowager countess from *Downton Abbey*. I had to pass and it killed me.

But happily, as a result of training for the possibility of being a musical Joe Gillis, I had found a secret weapon to get my vocal cords in order. So now that I was on my way to the London stage for real, I decided to train for *A Few Good Men* as if it were a musical. If I could sing the show for eight performances a week, clearly I'd be able to speak it.

I remembered that back in the eighties, my pal Belinda Carlisle, of the Go-Go's, used a vocal coach who was a cantor at Los Angeles's biggest synagogues by day and voice coach to lead singers by night. I made an appointment to see Cantor Nathan Lamb.

For weeks, the cantor and I met at his temple office. He ran me through the same training that he used on his clients who had to sing to huge arenas night after night. We did scales. We did breathing drills. We worked on diction. But mostly, we worked on power. By the time I hit the Royal Haymarket stage, my speaking voice could bounce back to me from the farthest wall of the highest balcony. I was ready.

But first, I took Sheryl and the boys on a vacation—we landed in London on the morning of July 7, 2005. Arriving at baggage claim, the exiting passengers were met with a phalanx of terse-lipped, ashen-faced airline reps.

"The airport is on lockdown. No further flights in or out."

Only text messages got us the news that was breaking just miles away: London had been attacked by terrorists. Fifty-two innocent people had been blown to bits by suicide bombers. The city braced for more.

By renting a car and driving to another airport, we eventually managed to escape London, but we returned for the first day of rehearsals two weeks later. The city was still on edge. Tourism had plummeted. Sheryl and I talked about the wisdom of moving our young family to a city so on the brink.

"I think the main threat is over," I told her, without any evidence to back up my theory. "We'll be safe."

We moved into a beautiful flat on Eaton Terrace in Belgravia. I wanted my family comfortable while they supported me, so far from home.

Rehearsals took place in a steamy, dusty sweatbox and I loved every minute of it. After a full day of scene work or even after a full run-through, I always wanted to stay to work more. Aaron was right there with me. Minus the pressure-cooker personality parade that was *The West Wing*, *A Few Good Men* was easy, fun, fulfilling and focused solely on making something the best it could be.

Shortly before our opening, at our press conference in front of all of London's media, I was asked if I ever thought of pulling out due to the 7/7 bombings.

I told them no.

"Look, on 9/11 and after, you guys had our backs. Now it's our turn. I'm happy to be able to support London. I feel safe here, 'cause let's face it, when it comes down to it, no one is tougher than the British."

The next day, back in our rehearsal hellhole, I was standing in my underwear doing a fitting when our stage manager approached.

"Um, Mr. Lowe, you have a visitor."

Figuring it was Sheryl, I threw on a towel and headed out of the changing room.

"Sir! You'd better put on some clothes," he called. I noticed he was shaking.

I put my jeans and shirt on and walked into the rehearsal hall. Some of the actors were there looking around anxiously. No one spoke. The front door opened and my visitor arrived. It was the prime minister, Tony Blair.

He walked toward me with a smile, like we'd been friends forever.

"Rob! What a pleasure!" he said.

"Mr. Prime Minister!" I managed to say through my shock. I went to shake his hand, but he pulled me in close for a hug.

"I wanted to come and thank you for what you said about our country," he whispered. He looked at me with a sincerity that deeply touched me. I was taken aback by his gratitude and warmth. A moment later, he was gone. His visit was never made public.

I truly believe that anyone can be good and possibly even great acting in movies or TV. Obviously, to be *consistently* good requires a true actor, but with the army of people involved in making a film actor successful, even a loaf of bread could deliver a decent performance. You have multiple takes, you have directors to guide you and an editor to cut to you (or away from you) as needed. There are some actors whom editors cut away from multiple times on the same line of dialogue! (Start looking for that, you'll notice it more than you think.)

Not so onstage. It's all you. You can't make the viewer look elsewhere when you want, you can't take a plodding scene and sex it up with fancy cutting. You can't hold people's attention with anything but your own work. You have no second chances; it's you, and only you, in the driver's seat. It's lonely and it's exhilarating. Those who do it well are acting's true professionals.

You can't go onstage without being functional in the craft of the theater. And besides vocal ability, the number one area to be mastered is, not surprisingly, memorization. For film acting, you can play fast and loose with memorizing. Forget a line and it may be slightly embarrassing, but everyone does it and you just do another take. Forget your lines onstage and you have a serious problem.

I've been memorizing lines the same way I did when I was nine years old and appearing in local theater in Ohio. No one taught me, I had no special tips, I just did what I did through trial and error. Read the line, cover it with my hand, try to remember it, remove my hand and check my success. Pretty rudimentary, but this method got me through a lot of movies.

But when Sorkin casually mentioned that Kaffee has as many lines as Hamlet, I figured I better step up my game. I tried a method that Allison Janney used each day on *The West Wing*. Supposedly she picked it up from a friend who trained at the Royal Shakespeare Company. With this new method, I had this massive part down cold within three weeks, working every day in twenty-minute blocks, four or five times a day.

Here's how it works:

Take a piece of paper and pen. After reading the line you need to memorize, write the line out *using only the first letter of every word*. Include all punctuation. For example, here's Kaffee's big courtroom speech to Colonel Jessup that begins the famous "You can't handle the truth" sequence:

KAFFEE

Your Honor, these are the telephone records from GITMO for July 6th. And these are 14 letters that Santiago wrote in nine months requesting, in fact begging, for a transfer off the base.

(to Jessup)

Upon hearing the news that he was finally being transferred, Santiago was so excited, that do you know how many people he called? Zero. Nobody. Not one call to his parents saying he was finally getting out. Not one call to a friend saying can you pick me up at the airport. He was asleep in his bed at midnight, and according to you he was getting on a plane in six hours, and everything he owned was folded neatly in a footlocker and hanging neatly in a closet. You were leaving for one day and you packed a bag and made three phone calls. Santiago was leaving for the rest of his life, and he hadn't packed a thing, and hadn't called a soul. Can you explain that?

(pause)

The fact is, Santiago wasn't going anywhere, isn't that right, Colonel?

If you were to stumble during this one, the play would be over.

Here's how it should look using the memory technique:

KAFFEE
Y h, t a t t r f GITMO f J 6th. A t a 14 1 t S w i n m r, i f b, f a t o t b.

(to Jessup)

U h t n t h w f b t, S w s e, t d y k h m p h c? Z. N. N o c t h p s h w f g o. N o c t a f s c y p m u a t a. H w a i h b a m, a a t y h w g o a p i s h, a e h o w f n i a f a h n i a c. Y w l f o d a y p a b a m t p c. S w l f t r o h l, a h h p a t, a h c a s. C y e t?

(pause)

T f i, S w g a, i t r, C?

By writing it out you add an additional brain function. By reducing the word to one letter, you are programming your brain beyond what you would if you wrote the full word. When finished, you have a one-letter cue to help your memory, but your mind still needs to fill in the word. It is a perfect mix of being prompted and having to struggle. I found it reduces memorization time by half. At least.

Unfortunately, it didn't help me on opening night.

We had been whizzing through previews with full houses and a great response. The whole cast was on fire, and I was confident and ready for our opening, where, unlike Broadway, all the critics would come to that one performance (in New York they could attend any show during the preview period). This makes the stakes higher. The play's future is judged on one single show.

Weird, but good, things were happening all night. At one point the circular emblem on the judge's lectern fell to the stage with a loud thud in the middle of a scene. It then rolled ridiculously slowly all the way across the stage while both the cast and audience stared at it. I walked over, picked it up and reattached it in front of the judge.

"I believe this is yours, Your Honor," I ad-libbed. The audience applauded.

In the middle of the second act there was a moment that we had never quite executed. It was nothing overly dramatic, just a crisp exchange between me and the actor playing Corporal Kendrick. For the first time since we began rehearsing almost six weeks previously, he and I got it right. There was a nice reaction from the crowd. He and I stole a quick smile at each other.

This night of "happy accidents" going our way, I allowed myself a private moment of acknowledging how well the show was going. This while in the middle of a cross-examination scene.

When actors get too comfortable onstage, it can be dangerous. They are in peril of being on a kind of autopilot. You might suddenly think, "Oh shit! I forgot to call my brother back last night!" right in the middle of delivering a monologue. It is always a fatal mistake.

Suddenly I was aware of my fellow actor staring at me, pop-eyed. Beads of sweat sprouted across his brow. Quickly, I understood his horror. In the split second I had taken my mind off the scene, I had jumped almost *four pages* ahead! This was problematic because those four pages contained vital plot points crucial to the play's outcome. Although no one in the packed opening-night crowd knew it, I had just fucked up the entire show.

As it does in all horrifying events, time slowed to a crawl. My fellow actor's face was now drenched in sweat. Out of the corner of my eye I could see the rest of the cast in the courtroom, stealing glances at each other, trying to hide their rising panic.

Years ago, hosting *Saturday Night Live*, I blew the setup for a punch line that Phil Hartman had that would end our scene. Without the setup, there was no joke; without the joke there was no ending to the scene. We were live, and we were screwed. But the late, great Phil looked me in the eye like, "Dude. Easy does it. We got this," and guided me through an ad-libbed improv to an even better joke than the one that had been written. It took this near miss to learn an important lesson of acting live. The audience doesn't know you've screwed the pooch until you show them you have. So don't.

I gave the actor sitting in the witness box the look Phil Hartman gave me. I then stopped the scene cold and walked to the absolute front of the stage. Now I could *really* feel the other actors trying not to freak out. I milked the moment; I let the silence play out until it was painful. I used the time to plot my way back into the scene, to focus on the story points I needed to get to. But because I did it with purpose and confidence, making this long beat part of my performance, it played.

"Mr. Kendrick, I want to take a moment to circle back on a few items."

"Yes, sir."

Then, slowly, I wove my way back to the text. Soon I had folded all the information needed into my improv. I could tell that no one in the house had any clue about what had happened.

"No further questions, you may step down," I finished, turning away from the audience and facing my upstage cast mates. I made a cartoon face of "Holy fucking shit!" to them as I approached, but I was also feeling that unique adrenaline-fueled victory that only comes from competing in the public arena. I felt even better when I learned that Sorkin had missed the whole thing. He was calming his nerves with a cigarette at the time, which will go down in history as the world's most healthy smoke. Because sitting through my line-bungle adventure would've given him a heart attack.

You really do see it all during a long run of a show in the theater. Not just blown cues but other things as well.

Apparently, it is well-known within the West End theater community that there is a notorious couple that likes to have sex right there in the audience. I had originally called bullshit on this tale, figuring it was a chance for the all-British cast to "have a go" at the Yankee interloper.

Then came a rudimentary midweek matinee.

In the better theaters in London, there is always a special, private box reserved for the queen. Most of the time it is either empty or sold to VIPs. On this particular day I noticed in passing that it was occupied by an attractive young couple (I was always aware of who was in the house for any given performance).

Somewhere around the time where Kaffee and the gang go to

Cuba to first meet Colonel Jessup, I noticed something going down in the queen's box. Literally.

While trying to concentrate on the actor standing in front of me, I noticed that there was now only the man sitting in the box. A moment later a blond female head rose out of his lap, above the gilded wall separating them from the rest of the house. Then she dove back below to continue her performance, which was unquestionably more interesting than anything we were attempting onstage.

At the intermission the couple was told in no uncertain terms that this particular behavior was not tolerated within the confines of the queen's box at the Theatre Royal Haymarket. The randy couple swore they would not do it again. And so they were allowed to stay.

They kept their word. They never did repeat that particular act. Like the play itself, after intermission, they were building to a climax, and the final courtroom showdown featured me bellowing, "I want the *truth!*" while the supposedly chastened couple rode each other like the *Urban Cowboy* mechanical bull. Luckily, by the end of the show they were gone; I wouldn't have wanted to find out who would've gotten a bigger curtain call.

Speaking of curtain calls, my time in the UK showed me some profound differences between American and British theatergoers. In America, audiences are vocal and ready to be pleased. They give out standing ovations like Halloween candy. In fact, I haven't seen a show in New York in twenty years that didn't include one. On Broadway, you will also have wrappers ripping, loud food eating and at least four or five ringing cell phones a week. I never heard *one* in over 160 performances in London. But we were also light on standing ovations. Maybe ten the whole run. If you eked one out of those respectful but demanding British crowds, you knew you had really earned it, and it was special. In spite of my four-page fuckup, the first and loudest one we got was on opening night.

———

Prepping for a role, fashioning a character, is sometimes a give-and-take between actor and director. But not always. Good actors learn early to protect themselves from inexperienced (or bad) directors by taking the care and feeding of their performances into their own hands. We make choices that force editors to cut to us when we want (light a cigarette on an important line or take off or put on your glasses, and they have to show it) or make other choices we know they can't use, so the focus will be on some other poor slob. Good actors almost always know how to get cut to in a scene. And hack actors, unfortunately, use those tricks mercilessly. One of the things I've always admired about the cast of *The West Wing* is that everyone was too proud to stoop to that style of acting. The kind that says, "Cut to me! I'm *listening*! I'm *reacting*!" By this I mean behavior that is not found in nature but only in bad TV shows or movies. It's nodding your head "sagely" while being told a story. It's "stealing a glance" at a third party while you listen. It's checking your watch at the defense table during closing arguments. It's feeling like you have to *do something* while the camera is on you when you are not talking. In *The West Wing*, we never did. We just listened. Like people do. In real life.

The better your collaborators, the more you want to collaborate. Recently I worked with Steven Soderbergh, who is truly a master of every genre. He's done quirky, small, indie (in fact he practically invented the modern indie genre with *Sex, Lies, and Videotape*), he's done mass Hollywood blockbuster. He's done movies in space stations and male strip clubs. His movies have voice, vision and smarts, and are always slyly funny. This is a director you are happy to follow anywhere.

In *Behind the Candelabra* Michael Douglas plays Liberace, and Matt Damon plays his dimwitted, deer-in-the-headlights young gay lover. They are genius. I had always been a fan of both, Michael's *The American President* and Matt's *The Talented Mr. Ripley* being among my favorite performances by any actors. But nothing could've prepared me for the spectacle of seeing Jason Bourne giving a hummer to Gordon Gekko. Like I said, Steven Soderbergh is a master of many genres.

Some characters require more shaping than others. Some come fully formed, whether by the quality and specificity of the writing or from the role being based on a real person. Then it's more about research and authenticity than invention from whole cloth. When I played wife killer Drew Peterson, a doughy, mustached cop with a distinctive Chicago accent, the character was there for the taking. You couldn't have made him up. The real challenge was making me look like him. Luckily, there were hundreds of hours of footage of Peterson. Within them were direct quotes that were outrageous, priceless gems, like when he was asked where his missing wife was: "I dunno. I wish she'd pop her head up." I put these lines into the script or ad-libbed them whenever possible. I spent weeks listening to Peterson's voice. By the time I got to the set I could channel him.

Looking like him, however, was more difficult. I took the role because I had *no idea* if I could be believable in a character so far from who I am and what I look like. Any time an opportunity scares you that much, you should seriously consider saying yes.

The studio and network behind the movie weren't rushing to support my notion that to play Drew, I would need to totally transform. I had in mind some very cutting-edge prosthetics and dying my hair completely gray. They would've preferred a gentle frosting at the temples, a Selleck-like mustache and nothing else. "Selleck as Peterson" would've been the look. I often find, to my disappointment, that when the folks in the executive suites are paying for Rob Lowe they want me to look like Rob Lowe, regardless of who I'm playing. It's always a battle (which makes the success of my character in *Candelabra* that much sweeter).

After weeks of discussion and numerous screen tests, we all agreed on my Drew Peterson look. Surprisingly, turning my hair completely gray was the hardest part. Turns out there is no easy way to do it; as you can imagine there is not a huge market for it. The process took six and a half hours. First of all your own color is stripped out and then, in small increments, they work color back into the hair follicles bit by bit.

The day after I had my new hair, I was to meet Kate Middleton and the guy she was marrying from England, at a benefit in Santa Barbara. In the reception line, they were a dashing and charming couple, but he in particular couldn't take his eyes off of my white hair. I had hoped it would make me look dignified, like George Clooney. Instead I looked like the great-grandfather of George Clooney. "I can see Hollywood is treating you well," said the future king of England dryly.

Makeup on the set was done by makeup top gun Scott Wheeler. It took over two hours every morning. Special handmade appliances gave me Cowardly Lion–looking bags under my eyes; "plumpers" were attached to my teeth and gums to puff out my cheeks. And unknown to anyone else involved on the movie, I also wore a fake nose. I knew that the studio and network would never approve of me in a phony proboscis, but it was the final, necessary touch in the transformation. So I just did it. No one ever noticed, and it made all the difference. When the first photos of me in character leaked, they went viral. What could have been seen as a bad *Saturday Night Live* character look was instead greeted with stunned attention. Later, the movie itself would break ratings records.

So when *Behind the Candelabra* came my way, I knew the power of transformation. But would Soderbergh be supportive? I knew Michael and Matt were going to utterly change their appearance. Maybe my doing it as well would be overkill. It would be up to Steven. When you work with a master, you do what they say. Still, I had a pretty clear vision of my character, a seventies-era LA plastic surgeon.

"Steven, what's your appetite for me to really go for it with this character?" I asked him in our first phone call.

"Hey, do it! I'd love to see what you have in mind."

And there it is. The greats have no fear. They are open to all good ideas, wherever they may come from. They are secure enough in their experience and vision to give the people they've hired room to run.

The script described my role as a man whose face was so pulled and shiny, he looked like a doll. Growing up in LA, the only thing more disturbing than the earthquakes are the bad face-lifts. So I knew *exactly* how I wanted to look.

When finished, I looked like a transgendered Bee Gee. I realized that with my eyebrows yanked up so unnaturally (by a series of painful rubber bands taped to my skin and running around the back and top of my head), if I squinted, it looked especially freaky. Because in nature it is extremely hard to raise your eyebrows and squint at the same time. My "look" was set.

The character's voice was harder to figure out. In full makeup and wardrobe I looked very feminine. I knew the movie would be chockablock with fey characters, so I went in another direction. I imagined my guy as one of those countless transplanted New York wannabe tough guys who come to LA and end up going completely off the reservation. The kind of guys I see regularly at Lakers games. So I gave him a vaguely Brooklyn, gravelly-sounding rasp. If in *Pirates of the Caribbean* Johnny Depp was doing Keith Richards, in *Candelabra* I was doing the guy who used to do the Men's Wearhouse commercials.

The combo was enough that on the set, Matt Damon refused to look at me when the cameras were rolling. He would try not to laugh beholding this demented man I had conjured up. Sometimes tears would stream down his face. "Stop it," he would say, "I can't look at you!" Together, we had more fun than actors should be allowed to have.

I don't know why I enjoy playing weird-looking, depraved characters as much as I do. Maybe at this point in my life and career it's a nice palate cleanser from clean-cut optimists like Sam Seaborn on *The West Wing* or Chris Traeger on *Parks and Recreation*. Who knows. Maybe I shouldn't feel such glee when I show photos of my rogues' gallery to people and they react with "Eeew!"

In rehearsals for a role, there is inevitably one line that you hate, don't want to say and lobby to get cut. The late acting teacher Roy London always said of those lines, "The one line you don't want to say is usually the one you *must* say. It usually is a barrier you need to cross and often a gateway to a deeper understanding of your character." As much as I hate to relearn this with each project, I have to admit he's right.

In David Duchovny's dark and hilarious sex romp *Californication* I sometimes show up as Eddie Nero, a drug-addicted, pansexual loon who happens to be an Academy Award–winning movie star. Happily for me, I know a number of Eddie Neros personally. So playing Nero is one of my favorite treats. I get to send up everything I loathe (and, I suppose, love) about Hollywood stars. But in *Californication*'s extreme world of sex and language, there was one line in my first episode (with apologies to Roy London) that I simply was *not* going to say.

It was something about how, to research playing a gay hit man, Eddie "took a man in his mouth" and swallowed his "ropy jism."

"David, I love you, I love the show. I am *not* saying that!"

"Too much, ya think?" said Duchovny in his patented laconic monotone.

"Um, yes!"

"Hey, man. Sure. Whatever you want."

But the line was in my head and just as Roy promised, my obsessing on it led to a breakthrough. In its place I ad-libbed something that was arguably just as gross but that gave me a permanent hook into playing Eddie.

"I engineered that orgasm. I played his skin flute. I played his skin flute like Kenny G! Like Kenny G on ecstasy!" It became a much-quoted scene and can be seen in all its twisted glory all over YouTube.

Eddie Nero, and for that matter *Californication* itself, is not for everybody. I have advisers who are very smart who hate when I play characters who are meant to be divisive and provocative. And there are more than a few iconic careers that are bereft of even a single role that isn't a likeable hero. I mean, Will Smith turned down *Django Unchained* for God's sake. Redford (one of my heroes) never played a bad guy, and he certainly would never say he took a man in his mouth! At least not publicly, anyway. Those are two of the biggest and greatest stars who ever lived; they must be doing a lot of things right. But, to each his own; I can't help myself. When it comes to a great or scene-stealing role, I'm down, regardless of its sensibilities. For me, acting has never been about being popular or worrying about perception. And let's face it, it's always fun to be the bad boy.

Probably the first rake I ever played brought me some of my earliest cultural attention. Billy Hicks in *St. Elmo's Fire* became a role that had immediate and, for some, lasting impact. In the summer of 1985 you could see young dudes dressed as my character all over. In *Full House*, that era's popular sitcom, John Stamos most blatantly bit my character's look, but I was flattered. And today, people quote Billy's lines to me all the time.

The movie's director wanted me to have hair extensions. But due to my horrific inability to follow directions, I couldn't find the salon for my appointment and missed my window to get them put in. Or installed. Or whatever you call it. This was a true moment of God doing for me what I couldn't do for myself. One wrong turn saved me from having even *more* bad hair than I had in the movie anyway! Looking back, my do was one step away from a Phyllis Diller fright wig. Film historians attribute *St. Elmo's Fire*'s success to the burgeoning youth-in-film movement. I attribute the film's success to the invention of hair mousse.

To prepare for the part, I had to learn to play the saxophone. At that moment in time, my favorite musicians, Bruce Springsteen and the E Street Band, were just beginning their legendary Born in the USA Tour. I had recently met them all backstage at a concert in Toronto while making *Youngblood*. I went back a number of times, watched them and spoke to their iconic sax man, the late Clarence Clemons. The Big Man was gracious in sharing tips like what reeds to use in your sax and how to custom-rig the horn so you could throw it over your shoulder to look like a badass. In addition to this exclusive high-end tutorial from the most famous sax god on the planet, I also spent days with a playing coach learning how to properly "finger" the horn. It would take a few months to play with even a rudimental ability and we only had weeks. So the key was to learn to *look* like an expert. By the time we began shooting *St. Elmo's Fire* in late 1984, I could play some, but I could fake-play *a lot*. And I looked like a pro doing it.

A big reason it all came together for that movie was its music. My friend David Foster had written great songs for Michael Jackson, Earth, Wind & Fire, Chicago, Barbra Streisand and tons of other musical studs. For our movie he wrote "Love Theme from St. Elmo's Fire," which went to number fifteen on the charts, and "St. Elmo's

Fire (Man in Motion)," which was the massive number one hit of that summer. I fake-played my sax in both the film and the MTV music videos.

David became a good friend. He is a musical genius, funny and very brash. A perfect example: St. Elmo's was David's first crack at writing a major Hollywood movie score. He was, at the time, one of the record industry's most sought-after producers, working on multiple projects at once. In fact, as the deadline to write the score approached, he was also struggling to write a big charity anthem for a fellow Canadian, a paraplegic who was going to circle the world by wheelchair.

"I don't know which is harder, writing that kind of inspiration song or one that has to rhyme with the phrase 'St. Elmo's Fire,' " he told me.

In the end, he did both at the same time. Killing two birds with one stone, he took his song for Rick Hansen's "Man in Motion" wheelchair tour and merely added the phrase "St. Elmo's Fire" a few times. No one seemed to care that the film's number one hit song contained lyrics that had absolutely no connection to the movie whatsoever ("Gonna be your man in motion, all I need is a pair of wheels / Take me where my future's lyin', St. Elmo's Fire!").

David and I stayed in touch long after I stopped wearing earrings and using hair mousse, often running into each other at some of the high-end charity events that David was involved in. At a fund-raiser for then-president Bill Clinton, David had an idea.

"Since I'm the musical director tonight, I'll have to play the St. Elmo's love theme," he said, owing to the fact that, according to ASCAP, for a ten-year period more people were buried and married to his ditty than any other. "What if you played the sax solo like you did in the video?"

"Um, how exactly would that work?" I asked, seeing as how I'd never actually played it.

"I'll call you up from your table, I'll have a sax ready and you mime playing while the real sax player hides offstage."

The idea made me laugh. "Maybe I'll take a sip of water in the middle of the solo, like the old vaudeville-player piano joke where you 'mistakenly' reveal that it's all fake."

"Exactly. People will love it!"

I was inclined to agree. Even though the room would be packed with Los Angeles's A-listers, I figured even that kind of jaded crowd would appreciate the gag.

I told David I was in.

"Great. I will play it as the closing number, right after 'After the Love Has Gone.' "

I told Sheryl our plan. She is my number one sounding board and I always listen to her perspective.

"Don't do it," she said.

There is no one in the world who has her feel for the realities of life. Few have her keen business mind, facility for numbers or ability to connect with people. But she absolutely never wants to see me at risk, particularly when it comes to comedy, where the risk/reward ratio is higher than in any other genre. The very fact that Sheryl was uncomfortable with my doing the gag, to me, meant I had to do it. My only real hesitation was whether or not I still knew the solo well enough to sell it.

By the time David played his Earth, Wind & Fire hit, everyone was into it. At the next table, I could see President Clinton smiling and bobbing his head.

"I think my pal Rob Lowe is in the house," David said as he finished. "You out there, man?"

I raised my hand.

"I just had an idea! I don't mean to put you on the spot, but do you still know the solo from 'St. Elmo's Fire'?" he asked.

Before I could attempt to answer, people were clapping and egging me on.

Like those Academy Award winners who've won every single award leading up to the Oscars, I did my best "Well, I'm *shocked*! I'm just *so overwhelmed*! I'm *so surprised* to find myself in this situation!" act.

I demurely made my way to the stage, passing movie stars, national political figures and famous musicians. I passed Quincy Jones, who gave me a "good luck" wink. President Clinton looked on eagerly.

"There's no turning back now," I thought. I hoped I could still nail the song, but if I couldn't I'd just cut right to the joke of not really playing. I grabbed the shiny Selmer tenor sax waiting "conveniently" on a stand next to David's piano.

"I hope you don't fuck up!" he said. I looked out to Clinton, who laughed. David started to play.

It truly is a gorgeous song. I remember first hearing it in the editing room of the movie and tearing up. I watched David play and was swept up in memories that seemed from another lifetime. I snapped out of it as the big solo approached.

In a performance, it's the little details that bring authenticity. Knowing how many files a lawyer would carry into a closing argument is almost as important as delivering a good one. Adjusting your mouthpiece and wetting your reed with your tongue sells musicianship as much as anything else. So, I prepared my horn and walked downstage front for the solo.

The battle would be won or lost with the first note. When I took the big breath and blew, no sound would come out, as I'd moved the reed down in the mouthpiece. It would look great with my neck veins popping, but unless the man behind the curtain blew at *exactly* the same time, the jig would be up.

We hit the note in perfect time. Now we just had to do it with each note throughout. I also had to remember when to breathe in the right spots, but apparently it had become muscle memory, because my phrasing was spot-on. People were jumping to their feet and cheering. I was shocked that no one could tell that no sound was coming out as I blew like a hurricane.

I saw the president pumping his fist. From his seat just feet away from my silent horn, Quincy Jones was yelling, "Yeah, baby!" The thing was going down like a house on fire. I looked at Sheryl, who had her head in her hands.

It's at this point, with LA's glitterati going wild before me, that I lost the plot completely. I decided not to show that it was a joke. This thing was killing; people who I thought would've known better were *so* into it that I didn't dare pull the rug out from under them.

Even David was into it like we were live at Budokan. Every time I thought about taking my fingers off the horn and revealing the real player behind me, I just couldn't. I was as swept up as everyone else.

We finished to a huge ovation. You could see the shock on everyone's face that I could just get up from my table and put a beat-down on a song like that. I was in a daze as well as I made my way through the crowd.

"I had no *idea* you were a player!" said Quincy, grabbing me for a hug.

Back at my table, Sheryl shook her head sort of like my mom used to do after I pulled some stunt on one of my brothers.

I looked up and caught President Clinton's eye. He was grinning from ear to ear and doing the *Wayne's World* "We're not worthy!" gesture.

Driving home, I was feeling both elated and a little guilty. I was happy that I'd been able to give a surprising bit of entertainment to such a tough crowd. On the other hand, I felt a little bit like I'd unintentionally pulled a fast one on some people you don't really want to fool around with. Like the leader of the free world. But I told myself that all that mattered was that my bit with David went over huge and it would all be forgotten tomorrow anyway.

I was wrong. Two weeks later I received a handwritten note, on White House stationery, from President Clinton. It was a characteristically gracious thank-you for coming to his fund-raiser and an invitation to play a duet with him on the sax next time I was in DC. His note was so effusive about my phony-baloney sax skills that I felt a surge of Episcopalian guilt all over again.

"Rob. Get over it," I told myself. "What the president of the United States doesn't know won't hurt him!"

A few days later I got around to telling David Foster about my letter from Clinton. David was understandably thrilled.

"But I feel a little bad that he thinks I can actually play. I hope he never finds out that we were just fooling around."

"He already has," said David.

"Whaaat?"

"Yeah, he knows you were faking it."

"What? How . . . how did he find out? Did you tell him?"

"No, of course not!" replied David.

"Who did?!"

"Barbra Streisand."

"Barbra Streisand? But . . . But . . . How would *she* know? She wasn't even *there!*"

"I told her."

"You *what*?!"

"Well, we were in the studio together a few days ago and I told her about it. Apparently, she then called the president to tell him you were faking it."

If you've ever wondered what the correct definition of "first-world problems" is, wonder no more. I was now in a full shame spiral involving Barbra Streisand and the president of the United States.

Meanwhile, in reality, Sheryl was of little comfort. "I *told* you it was a bad idea!" she said.

Being nothing if not practical, and also having no patience for my grandiosity, she then gave me very sound advice:

"Rob, honey, I don't think the president of the United States is spending a lot of time thinking about you or your sax playing."

This is why I love my wife. She always calls it like it is; she is never afraid to tell me what I need to hear.

"Seriously, babe. Just let it go."

But I couldn't. Part of me was certain that Clinton would be burning up the phone lines to Streisand.

"You know, Barbra, I just can't get over this Rob Lowe hoodwinking!"

"I understand, Mr. President. I myself was disappointed to find he is one of Hollywood's leading assholes."

"Yes. How true. And what of that David Foster?"

"Oh, sir, David's a saint. I loved the song he wrote about that poor boy in the wheelchair. Anyway, I'm sure the whole thing was Rob Lowe's idea."

After more obsessing, I decided I had no choice but to try to explain myself to the president. So I wrote him a note.

In it, I basically said how much I appreciated his note to me and that it had come to my knowledge that perhaps there was a "misunderstanding" about my saxophone abilities.

"In the cold light of day, perhaps my playing is not what it would appear. That said, I would still love to duet with you. We just need a third player behind a curtain!" it read. One of the gifts of *The West Wing*'s legacy is having a few back channels directly to the Oval Office. I gave the note to a trusted emissary, longtime California congressman David Dreier, who was seeing the president the following week.

Congressman Dreier delivered my note. I didn't expect a reply and got none. Happily, I've seen the president since and all seems well. I'm now certain that Sheryl was right as usual and Clinton had a laugh about it with Streisand and moved on to things of slightly more importance, like Iranian nukes. But that evening was a good lesson that performances on a big stage can quickly go awry and that there is sometimes no true way to quantify how far an actor will go to win over a crowd.

It's also a happy reminder that if you are lucky, over many years as a performer you will have developed many abilities and wonderful tools to use at your pleasure, as an actor prepares.

JFK in *Killing Kennedy.*

Dr. Jack Startz in *Behind
the Candelabra.*

Drew Peterson in *Untouchable:
The Drew Peterson Story.*

Chris Traeger in *Parks and
Recreation.*

Eddie Nero in
Californication.

My rogues gallery. Over a two-year period,
some very diverse characters.

Change, in the New World

As a typical Midwestern kid, my view of the entertainment industry (and I would never have known that term) was that of most people outside of Hollywood. Which is to say that I was bereft of any sophistication about the peculiarities and sometimes-nonsensical foibles inherent in a business where artists are in constant conflict with bean counters and where bad behavior is often rewarded as long as it fills seats. I would never have guessed that Hollywood is the land where no good deed is not expected to be replicated again next time, exactly and for less money. (A perfect example being: Come in under budget and you are expected to make the next movie or episode for *that* new number, even if it has a much larger scope.) The war between art and commerce has always been fought, even in the days when I still thought *Battle of the Network Stars* had the same pedigree as the Super Bowl. Today, it's worse, as viewers flee the big networks and movies struggle to compete with new forms of entertainment.

Then and now, it's a miracle when anything really good gets made and even rarer that it isn't eventually destroyed by cost cutting. If you've ever wondered why your favorite show worsened a few seasons down the road, this is probably why.

I have tremendous sympathy for both sides. I am a producer as well; I get it. *Someone's* gotta mind the store. But it is inevitably a business that cannot be run through a spreadsheet. Making *Game of Thrones* or *The Walking Dead* or *American Hustle* is not like manufacturing widgets, no matter how much the boys upstairs would like it to be. It's a business predicated on human inspiration and passion, something that cannot be explicitly quantified in the bottom line, or micromanaged, or even really told what to do.

But in spite of it all, magic does happen. When I was a boy and I saw it on my TV or movie screen, I was driven ever closer to my dream of being a part of this glorious and maddening business.

I remember sitting with my family, watching *All in the Family* and even as a boy being taken aback at the hilarious but quasi-racist Archie Bunker. Today, I know that show could never be put on a network schedule. The way the Bunkers dealt with race alone would be too hot to touch in our PC culture. But back then, my family's week revolved around that magic half hour in front of our black and white Zenith. I vividly remember the first time I heard Edith talk in her real voice (like most showbiz civilians, unless an actor was known for multiple roles and a long career, I thought they *were* that first big role they became famous for). I remember seeing Edith—I'm sorry, Jean Stapleton—at what must have been the Emmys, looking beautifully sophisticated in her gown and speaking in a deep, resonant way that was as far from Edith as I was from Hollywood. There was not one shred of the dithering, shrill, slow-witted working-class housewife from Queens to be found in her real-life persona. Her character on the show was so original, so seamlessly believable and so boldly drawn that I'm sure I wasn't alone in thinking, "That's just who she is." But now I was forced to consider a new concept—that she was *acting*.

All unknown actors struggle to overcome the "gift" of that first breakout role. Some of them will not have the opportunity or the range to do it. But the really good ones will.

I did a movie with Jonah Hill. He had just blown up from *Superbad*, a movie that is even better than you think it is. We were on location in Boston and people would yell, "Hey, it's *Superbad*!" What's up, *Superbad*?!" I was envious of Jonah for having gotten the part of a lifetime but not at all envious of his having to move beyond it. I needn't have worried; within a few years Jonah had a number of signature roles and award nominations, and no one was calling him *Superbad*.

Every profession has its inherent pitfalls. Acting is no different. At the pro level, the farther you rise, the more you are going to be in conflict with the inherent disconnect between "show" and "business." One of the few great things about being a struggling actor is that no one cares about the artistic choices you make, or anything else you do for that matter. But when Viacom or Comcast or Disney is writing your paychecks, oftentimes they are going to want to have their say. This is absolutely fair; it's their money. Most of the time everyone coexists peaceably. But when it goes bad, it does so in a hurry, because unlike most businesses, the boss and the employee have two completely opposite worldviews. The owners of the studios and networks want to make a profit; their employees want to make "art." In my experience, the two concepts meet about 25 percent of the time. Unfortunately, too many executives and too many artists each distrust the ethos of the other; if they could meet one another halfway in terms of the product they make, I believe the success level could be more like 40 percent.

Businessmen often distrust artists, and often for good reason. Another childhood favorite of mine was the show *Alias Smith and Jones*. With today's perspective I would've known it was a blatant rip-off of the recent hit movie *Butch Cassidy and the Sundance Kid*, but as a little boy I loved it and found it totally original. And when my favorite actor, Pete Duel, who played Jones, blew his brains out, ending the show, I was devastated. I didn't even know what suicide was. And a concept that I'm sure the suits at Universal weren't looking to sell to ten-year-olds across America was nevertheless brought into my living room courtesy of a deeply troubled actor.

With one sad and tragic act, a franchise was lost, scores were out of jobs and millions of the studio's dollars were gone. Creative people are often their own worst enemy when it comes to commerce. I've seen a number of charismatic, talented, funny and great-looking leading men break apart on the shoals of insisting on playing only destitute, drug-addled, eighteenth-century quadriplegic Irish poets. It's true that every once in a while you need to shock people, but Cary Grant had no issue with always wearing the same dark suit and haircut and he did just fine. The fact that he never won an Oscar has nothing to do with his talent and everything to do with how easy he made it look, how good he looked doing it and how easily enraptured Oscar voters are with fake noses, phony accents and histrionic acting. Also, it didn't help that Cary was funny. They don't give Oscars to funny people. Today, more than ever, when comedies are one of the few reliably profitable genres and the Oscars are even more about pushing product, you'd think at some point someone funny would end up at the podium. Don't hold your breath. It's one of the clearest examples of the great and growing disconnect between what the public is interested in and what the Hollywood establishment wants to recognize as "good."

The story that perhaps best illustrates the conflict between artists and their benefactors is the famous David Geffen–Neil Young lawsuit. Geffen had been Young's comanager for years and signed him to record two albums for his new label, obviously hoping to continue a brilliant catalog containing everything from "Old Man" and "Cinnamon Girl" to "Heart of Gold" and "Like a Hurricane." Instead, Neil recorded one album where he sang through a mechanical voice box like a robot or Woodstock-era Daft Punk member and another where he appeared like Roy Rogers on the cover while doing swing band/ western mash-ups. The lawsuit accused Neil Young of "making albums that were not characteristic of Neil Young." Which is obviously both true and not true. An artist has every right to create whatever they want (especially a genius like Neil), but you can imagine Geffen's frustration at underwriting Young's debut as R2–D2.

I've never really understood why anyone would be drawn to the entertainment business who wasn't an entertainer in some form. Without the emotional payback of creating, I would flee show biz quickly indeed. I wouldn't willingly choose an endeavor that trades so heavily on fear, lemming-think and doublespeak. I'm always amazed and a little sad when I meet a parent who tells me that their son or daughter "wants to get into the business." The statement itself is faulty on its face; what goes on daily in Hollywood bears absolutely no resemblance to any business whatsoever. I cannot think of another enterprise where you can't get principals on the phone when a multimillion-dollar decision hangs in the balance or that shuts down completely from a week before Thanksgiving to a week after New Year's (this seven-week period is called "the holidays"). It is also increasingly a business that has no memory of why it can be great—you can routinely bring up fairly obvious classic film references and be met with silence. Unfortunately, on the other side of the desk, more and more, the goal isn't to make *Network* or *Bringing Up Baby*, it's to make your quarter numbers and get promoted to run the jet engine division of your parent company.

Counterintuitively, in a business that should be based on the written material it makes (or chooses not to), few actually do any reading. And I'm not talking about *Atlas Shrugged* or the lesser works of Jerzy Kosinski; I'm talking about the scripts they are actually considering making into movies or television shows. Instead, many rely on the industry's version of CliffsNotes.

There exists, in Hollywood, a thing called "coverage." This is an extremely condensed version of the script: plot points, characters, tone, genre and truncated synopsis of the story. Coverage is put together by readers employed by whoever does not want to read the actual script. Usually people who are on the front lines of trying to discern which ones are viable, agents and studio executives. These "readers" are often unpaid interns just out of USC film school, or perhaps a newly hired agent's assistant. Sometimes coverage is farmed out on a script-by-script basis to people who do nothing but create coverage. As opposed to creating actual movies or TV shows. And the last element in the process is the opinion of the coverage creator. They do a full-on Pauline Kael–meets–Irving Thalberg recommendation on whether the script should be made. Most of the time if a script's coverage is anything less than glowing, oftentimes based on the opinion of someone who is writing from a Starbucks with spotty Wi-Fi and has never stepped foot on a movie set, it is DOA.

Can you imagine the number of great things that would've never been made in other businesses if they got bad coverage? If the "deciders" (as G. W. Bush would say) went on the opinions of interns working for free in, for example, architecture and construction? I can imagine coverage on the plans to build the Lincoln Memorial. It might read something like this . . .

PROPOSED PROJECT

TITLE: The Lincoln Memorial

Terrible title, completely unimaginative. Maybe Lincoln's Lair? Or possibly Dome of the Great Emancipator? (Although the plans submitted are not that of a dome.)

STRUCTURE: Poor

It is heavy, portentous and overwrought. It feels dated. One seems to be drowning in limestone (which hasn't worked as a popular building material since the WPA era).

DESIGN: Not very good at all.

You can't even *see* Abraham Lincoln from the street! Also, there are way too many stairs to climb to get to him. We need to see Abraham Lincoln much earlier. He is the star!

The blueprint submitted for our approval also shows a profound lack of understanding of what works in the marketplace. Exhausted stair-climbers do not want to enter a huge, dimly lit room and crane their necks to look *up* to see the statue. The Lincoln statue should be at our audience's eye level. Also, his hands are too large and completely unrealistic. Everyone knows Lincoln was not thirty feet tall. Looking at this plan, I did not even *once* think I was looking at the real Abraham Lincoln.

I also hated the words on the walls. Way too serious, and a little depressing. People don't want to hear about dead soldiers and slaves. Can't it be funnier? Or maybe keep the slaves and soldiers on just one wall and come up with some of Lincoln's jokes on the other?

COMMENTS: I think the designer was going for a majestic, dramatic and somberly emotional testament to a human being who faced godlike problems. I suppose you could make a case for those themes, but would the public really be interested in that? I don't recommend you actually take the time to review the Lincoln Memorial. **PASS.**

Meanwhile, I can also imagine things I love and that *did* get made receiving bad coverage.

PROPOSED PROJECT

TITLE: *Sesame Street*

First of all, the title is misleading and dangerous. It brings to mind a road made of extremely hard-to-eat nuts. This being a proposed children's television show, I don't think it should be named after both a choking hazard *and* a very unsafe place for kids to play.

SUMMARY: I found the show's setting troubling. Why would young children be happy about playing among urban tenements? The show should be reimagined in the suburbs, at a grassy park, with many trees. No one is interested in manholes.

The writer shows a complete lack of discipline by creating an extraordinarily inconsistent vision of the characters. Some are humans and some are puppets! If there are to be puppets, the world should be a total puppet world. Anything else is confusing and possibly frightening. Especially to children.

I found the tone misanthropic. One of the main characters is even named Oscar the Grouch. (I did like some of his dialogue, however. Perhaps just rename to Oscar the Great?)

I was also thrown by the descriptions of the adult characters. One is a young, idealistic black man; one is an old, kind, Jewish store owner and still others are identified as white, Chinese and American Indian. It is a confusing cultural hodgepodge. Young children are free to roam unaccompanied without supervision; these disparate cultures blend seamlessly in harmony and goodwill, while the characters act as mentors and friends to the children. This is completely unrealistic and unlike any neighborhood in the real world. Children are impression-able. We need not expose them to relationships and experiences they are unlikely to have in their own lives. Recommendation: **PASS**.

In spite of this system, obviously gems still get made. But more and more I feel this is in spite of it rather than because of it.

Behind the Candelabra is a perfect example. Written by Richard LaGravenese, one of Hollywood's handful of top guns, it was a movie no one wanted to make. Everyone said no. It was "too gay" or "about a star who kids don't remember" or whatever. Even with Steven Soder-bergh directing and two A-listers, Matt Damon and Michael Douglas, no studio would touch it. Even at a rock-bottom budget. For a long while it languished until the producers gave up on its being a theatri-cal movie and took it to TV, for HBO, and they said yes (although in the rest of the world it did play in theaters). This is another clear indication that television is *the* inevitable future destination for the bulk of smart, unique entertainment.

Behind the Candelabra, considering its pedigree and tiny budget, one would have thought, was a small bet worth taking. HBO said yes, and that's why it was nominated for eighteen Emmys instead of eighteen Oscars.

It's a new world. Change in all our lives and our business, what-ever it may be, is inevitable. One can bitch about it, like I just did, or suck it up and roll with the tide, as I always try to. There is almost al-ways an unforeseen silver lining to frustrating and demoralizing new barriers. *Candelabra* didn't get to be a studio movie, but more people saw it on TV in America than ever would have seen it in a movie theater. Although I enjoyed being a part of its success, what was most comforting was its reinforcement of what I sometimes struggle to re-member: Sometimes you can beat the system and a chorus of no's is rendered irrelevant by a single yes.

As a caveman, with Jonah Hill in a lost scene from *The Invention of Lying*.

Visiting one of my favorite places.

Just Do It

There came a point when the water of Long Island Sound began leaking into my small raft at such a rate that I began to consider what my obituary might say. The wild-eyed young production assistant, whom I had bribed to row me out to the middle of the bay for a clandestine rendezvous with a seaplane, fumbled with his walkie-talkie.

"Do you have Rob out there?" a voice I recognized as that belonging to the director of the movie I was attempting to flee asked with panicked suspicion.

"Don't answer him," I ordered, and handed the kid another $20.

"Is number one with you?!" he demanded, using the slang term for the star of a movie, based on the actor's top position on the day's call sheet.

I shook my head at the kid vigorously. "Just be cool. Don't respond."

I needed to find this seaplane. We were bobbing around, whitecaps rising and slopping over the rubber bulwark. If it didn't appear soon, my cohort and I would either be rousted by someone from the movie or be forced into the swirling, choppy drink.

"I . . . I . . . have to say *something*," said the PA. I realized he was probably right. And I didn't want to get him into any more trouble than he was clearly in already.

"Okay, tell them that they're breaking up and you can't really hear them. Tell them you'll be back right away."

As I had been lying flat and hiding under a blanket like a defector from East Berlin, I was confident the kid would be fine if he stuck to his guns and didn't crack under the questioning, which would surely be fairly intense, as the production discovered that I was indeed AWOL.

I hadn't meant it to become such an ordeal. It was 1987 and my beloved Los Angeles Lakers were locked in an epic, rigorous conflict with their loathed, bitter rivals, the Boston Celtics, for the NBA championships. I was a courtside season ticket holder and never missed a game. When I was on location, the Lakers front office would send Jack Nicholson and me tapes of our missed games via FedEx. Sometimes I even went on the road for important matchups. And there was none more important than game four in the dreaded Boston Garden.

Happily, I was a mere forty minutes away by air. I was making a movie (*Masquerade*) and although I was done for the week, the producers, knowing my Purple and Gold loyalty, had forbidden me from traveling to Boston. If something went wrong and I missed my return flight, I could've driven back in time for shooting, but they didn't care. Faced with such an indefensible and draconian house arrest in the Hamptons, I planned my escape.

We were shooting on the gorgeous but logistically challenging Shelter Island. I had missed the last ferry and was stranded. The seaplane was to meet me as soon as I wrapped at East Hampton Airport to make the tip-off. I had no time to waste. I had the plane rerouted to Shelter Island, but the charter company had been having a hard time relaying the new coordinates to the pilot, who had been circling over the set, tipping the plane's wings and waving his arm out the window.

"Do you know anything about this?" shouted my producers.

"Nope," I said.

I could tell that they didn't believe me, but without proof their only option was to shoot it out of the sky.

I ran back to my trailer and picked up my state-of-the-art Motorola "brick" cell phone.

"Please get that thing away from the set!" I'd begged the hapless charter representative. "Put it down out on the water. I'll meet it on Long Island Sound."

Now, as I began to bail water out of the raft, I saw no sign of the plane. Had it gotten the message? Did it mistakenly return to the airport? Should I head for shore and miss the game or should I risk drowning for the home team?

This wouldn't be the last time my youthful pre-sobriety enthusiasm and Laker love would put me in a pinch.

In the 1988 finals against the "bad boys" from Detroit, after benevolently attempting to share the wealth and sending some eager, loitering and pretty fans up to the players' rooms, I was banned from the hotel by Pat Riley. In that era, it was common to have a wonderful contingent of local supporters waiting to greet me in the lobby at most hours. I knew how lonely the road could be and wanted to do what I could to help the boys from Showtime (the team, not the network) have some needed R and R. Coach Riley was not amused. In fact, he took it out on me later during an unspeakably competitive and grueling match on Emilio Estevez's beach volleyball court, where he crushed me like a peasant uprising. The dude standing in front of the tank in Tiananmen Square met a better fate.

Back in LA for the same Detroit final, I hosted one of the Lakers stars at Mr. Chow after a Sunday victory. In those days I played for serious keeps when I was between movies, and I never considered that my Laker pal still had some big fish left to fry in the series. After trying to keep up with me into the wee hours, he returned to the Forum and promptly went into a career-low shooting slump that continued *into the next season.*

I'm glad Riley never got wind of that one.

Had I actually drowned attempting to flee the set of *Masquerade*, my Laker pal might've had better stats. But eventually I did secretly meet up with the seaplane and even made it to my seat in the Garden for tip-off. Perhaps as a Beantown welcome, I was seated next to notorious Laker hater and towel-waving former Celtic enforcer M. L. Carr. Every time I rose to my feet for Magic and company, old M. L. stared me down with hostile intent.

Earvin, who sees everything both on the court and off, sent his right-hand man, Lon Rosen, to change my seat at halftime, sparing me the wrath of Carr and the relentless heckling from the Celtic enthusiasts surrounding me.

The game was looking like a blowout, with the Celts up by fourteen. I had been placed high above the arena in the owner's box. It was so far above the court, and also so close to it, that you could look directly down through the center of the hoops, giving you a surreal angle on the action.

"Sorry about the score, Rob. Looks like it's over," said one of the Boston brass.

"Mmmm. I wouldn't count on it," I replied, and meant it, in spite of the odds of that kind of a comeback happening on an opponent's court in a game of that import.

And with that, Michael Cooper took an outlet pass and raced uncontested downcourt. Instead of an easy dunk, he pulled up and buried a long three. One of the greatest comebacks in NBA history followed, and the stage was set for one of the most memorable and replayed shots in all of sports.

In the steaming heat of the rat-infested Garden, the greatest point guard who will ever play the game took a pass directly beneath me on the close sideline. Five seconds on the clock, Lakers down by one. Magic Johnson, one of the NBA's all-time assist leaders, looked for the open man as he wheeled to the top of the key. Having watched hundreds of Lakers games, I recognized his body language: he was going to the hole himself. Robert Parrish and Kevin McHale, both seven-footers, closed the lane, arms outstretched, a dual ten-foot barrier. There was now no shot to be had, but Magic had committed.

"No no no no no!" I yelled, certain a rejection or turnover was imminent, and with it, probably the end of the championship series.

Magic picked up the dribble and as all of Lakerland groaned, forgetting in our anxiety exactly who we were dealing with, number thirty-two then unveiled a shot I had never seen him attempt in his career, *ever*. Including in warm-ups.

His old-school "baby" hook shot froze the building, arched over the twin seven-footers and fell like the dagger it was, through the net and into the hopes of the men in green.

Lakers by one.

Larry the Legend took a wide-open corner jumper (and from my top-down view it had a real chance) but missed. Perhaps the greatest NBA finals game was over. I looked for my Celtic hosts but they had already fled the scene of the crime.

Thank God for that seaplane; it had all been worth it.

Back on the set, they had apparently seen me at the game on television. They were not pleased that I misled them, but I wasn't late for work so it was a nonissue. I would've done it again in a second.

Adventure is important in life. Making memories matters. It doesn't have to be a secret seaplane and a historic sports moment, but to have a great life you need great memories. Grab any intriguing offer. Say yes to a challenge and to the unknown. Be creative in adding drama and scope to your life. Work at it like a job. Money from effort comes and goes, but effort from imagination and following adventure creates stories that you keep forever. And anyone can do it.

They don't have to be Hollywood-style, famous-person-cast, big events, either. The snapshots of my life I relive the most aren't.

My brother Chad and I have been obsessed with Bigfoot since we saw the B-movie *The Legend of Boggy Creek* at the Sidney, Ohio, movie theater as little kids in the seventies. In my area of Ohio, in those days and even later, when I would return for the summers as a teenager, there were movies and songs that were huge that my friends back in California never heard of. Movies like *Billy Jack*, *Emperor of the North* and *Dirty Mary Crazy Larry* and songs like "Billy Don't Be a Hero" and "The Devil Went Down to Georgia," which to this day I've never heard on the radio in Los Angeles. The Archies' "Sugar, Sugar" was such a sensation in the Buckeye State that you would've thought it was "Hey Jude." It is still the Ohio State marching band's go-to barnburner. Growing up in this unique and sometimes bizarre entertainment microclimate left me with a predilection for one-hit wonders, catchy bubblegum pop hits and . . . Bigfoot.

The plot of *The Legend of Boggy Creek* is foggy to me and that's probably for the best. I can't imagine the movie has aged well. But my seven-year-old self (what's left of him) still remembers the source of the "legend," a frightening "skunk ape," a below-the-Mason-Dixon version of Sasquatch. It blew my mind. I began to go to the library any chance I got to research Bigfoot. (Side note: Has there *ever* been a more horrific barrier to reading than the Dewey Decimal System? No wonder libraries are becoming irrelevant.) I took notes on all sightings and kept them in a green, semirusted, tin three-by-five recipe holder I purloined from my mother. I came across it recently, still intact after all these years.

Here is a typical entry:

"Willow Creek, California. Mutipul sightings. Footprints left. 10 to 12 foot creature. Threw logs and pushed over an engine."

Clearly, I was a little rubbery in my spelling but a little ahead of my time in my interest. Today, "Bigfoot hunting" is the new "Nazi hunting," the go-to programming staple of much of cable television's lesser networks. It's comforting to know that if the acting police finally apprehend me, I could still make a living as a telegenic Sasquatch hunter. The "Scud Stud" of bipedal-hominoid fetishists, if you will.

I tried to pass my interest on to my sons when they became the same age as I was when I saw *The Legend of Boggy Creek*. Both Matthew and Johnowen had an inherent interest in spooky things as well as an appreciative enthusiasm for the tall tales I would concoct at bedtime. Although I read them (and tried unsuccessfully to hide my tears over) *Where the Red Fern Grows* and the never-ending Harry Potter books, I most enjoyed my ad-libbed stories. As you can imagine, Bigfoot was a very useful character. Sometimes I would attempt to fashion a sort of multimedia experience by referring to goodies I found on the Internet.

As it turns out, one of the most famous recordings of a Bigfoot howling was made not far from where I grew up. "The Ohio Scream" is a truly frightening snippet of a bizarre-sounding, high-pitched shriek ending in a low, moaning wail. Authentic or not, it will make the hair on your neck stand up. Being the inveterate mimic I am, it wasn't long before I had my own version of the Ohio Scream. While

the boys enjoyed a scary bedtime story or two, I wasn't looking to trau-
matize them, so I kept my latest character under wraps. I believe that
all parents, however on point they may be, will, in the course of their
child-raising duties, give their kids plenty of ammo for the shrink's
couch, but I wasn't going to make my Bigfoot thing one of them.

But then the family planned a trip to the Pacific Northwest.

It was during Christmas break on my first year on *The West Wing*.
Having never been on an hour-long television series, I was already an
exhausted husk of a man and we had thirteen more episodes still to
do. And probably only an exhausted husk of a man would've agreed
to the itinerary my well-meaning and adventure-minded wife had put
together.

The plan was for us to join her sister Jodi; Jodi's husband, Brian;
and their two boys in a Winnebago caravan for a road trip up the
coast, camping in remote campsites as we went. This would be a
low-tech, old-school endeavor. I love to drive and I wanted my boys
to have the same "Are we there yet?" odyssey that I had as a child.

I have my strong suits and long ago stopped beating myself up
for my lack of facility in areas that aren't in my wheelhouse. For example, I am not what you would call "handy." I can't fix anything if
it breaks. I will never work for NASA. I will never even properly set
my DVR. Although I could change a flat tire if I had to, it wouldn't
be pretty and it would likely take a number of days. Thankfully, my
brother-in-law would be with us. He is not only unbelievably handy
but a teamster captain as well. Between the two of us, I would handle
the campfire stories, and he would make sure everything ran like a
military operation.

In Hollywood, Western Costume is the place all movies and TV
shows go to when stumped trying to find fantastic wardrobe. So naturally, I knew exactly where to go to find the most realistic Bigfoot

costume. I found a genuine-looking and slightly frightening bodysuit, Velcro-ed up the back, with a sculpted headpiece and deep-set black eye sockets. My idea was to put it on at some point in the trip, to ensure that the boys had their own "Bigfoot sighting." I hid the thing in the bowels of the undercarriage of the motor home for the utmost secrecy, and off we went.

For Christmas I had gotten Sheryl and the boys matching state-of-the-art bicycles. We hooked them to the back of the RV for the trail rides through the towering sequoias, but I crushed them into pretzel shapes backing out of our driveway. Brian, who had a long history of shooting projects on location, laughed. "Actors should hang out in Winnebagos, not drive them."

The trip improved rapidly once we got out of our driveway. We played cards, listened to music, played "spot the license plate" and all of the other family road-trip games that are in the American tradition. I was in heaven. Sheryl and I had created exactly the simple family vacation we'd hoped for.

Somewhere just south of Eureka, our caravan pulled into one of those irresistibly cheesy log-cabin tourist traps. When I was my kids' age, it would have been a Stuckey's with warnings of its impending freeway exit every mile. I have no idea why horrible Native American tchotchkes and maple-log rolls could've made a seven-year-old so happy, but they always did.

Although this place was no Stuckey's, it did offer something even better. There was an entire section devoted to Bigfoot! They sold totems, postcards and Sasquatch stuffed animals. The boys loved it.

A pleasant, middle-aged woman rang up our purchases.

"See much of Bigfoot up here?" I asked with a chuckle and enough plausible deniability cloaking my interest.

"Not so much anymore," she said with matter-of-fact seriousness.

I looked for some sign that she was being cute or pulling my leg a little. But she clearly meant what she'd said; it was as if I'd asked her about the snowfall levels in the area.

Not so much anymore.

I *had* to get to the bottom of this.

"Um, what do you mean?" I asked casually, as I didn't want to spook her into clamming up.

"We don't see them much now." I waited for more explanation but none was coming.

"So . . . you *have* seen them?"

"Oh sure. Saw them a lot when I was a girl," she said with not much enthusiasm, like she was describing a family who had moved away. "Most times I would be alone, and I would smell the bad smell and one would be there. When I was thirteen I was getting clothes off the line at sundown and it came out of the woods to look at me."

"Whaaaaaat?!" I was thinking, but instead just said, "Cool."

"Yeah. I think there's been so many roads put in, so much building, that they went deeper in the woods."

I shook my head.

"We don't see them much anymore," she said, and handed me my change.

Lucas and Jacob, my nephews, were towheaded, rough-and-tumble kids right out of *Tom Sawyer*. They loved my boys and vice versa. Brian and I spent a good part of the trip teaching them all the finer points of football as we camped in the pines and redwoods at our final destination, the almost unbearably gorgeous Patrick's Point near the Northern California border. Sheryl and her sister Jodi made us nightly feasts, Brian played guitar and I told stories. I will remember us as we were then, forever.

As an adjunct to my storytelling, one night I decided to debut my Ohio Scream, which I had been perfecting in secret for a number of months.

Excusing myself to go to the bathroom, I stepped away from the campfire and walked into the forest.

"Uuuooowaaaaaah!"

"Uuuuooowaaaah!"

Cantor Lamb would've been proud; I was all diaphragm and vocal technique as my spooky shriek echoed off the redwoods through our campsite.

When I returned, the boys were wide-eyed and excited.

"Dad!! Dad!! You missed it!! We heard a Bigfoot!!"

"Are you sure?" I asked.

"I think I would know," said Johnowen with a self-satisfied smile.

His brother and their cousins nodded their heads in agreement.

Later that night, as Sheryl and I cozied up in the back sleeping area of the motor home she asked, "Are you sure this Bigfoot thing is a good idea?"

"Absolutely!"

"Well, the cousins seemed a little freaked out."

"Ah, they're boys! It's good for them! All kids love scary campfire stories."

I could tell that she was not convinced and I chalked up our different views to yet another way that fathers and mothers see things differently. Which is good and the reason kids need both. One can say, "When you climb that jungle gym, be safe," while the other says, "Climb your highest."

The next morning I woke before anyone and stepped into the crackling frost covering the ground around our campsite. Soon everyone would be up exploring in the crisp December light, breath clearly visible but fading in the slowly warming sunshine. There was an unnamable satisfaction about it, about watching these boys together, observing them killing time, sometimes excited, sometimes bored, but always in nature and with very few distractions. I don't know why but I knew even as I was living those moments that they would ultimately be as unrepeatable as they were magical.

Secretly, I unearthed the Bigfoot costume from the luggage compartment under the RV. I inspected it closely for the evening's performance, as all actors should before going onstage. The suit was impressive, like the one in *Harry and the Hendersons*. The eyes in particular were quite good; they were dark marbles with irises that seemed to stare. The actual eyeholes were two diagonal slots below them, camouflaged with black netting. I rolled the thing up and hid it in the bushes for easy access that night.

After a long day of hunting the agates that peppered the rocky beach at Patrick's Point, we had a big dinner and broke out the s'mores at the campfire.

"Rob, did you see any Bigfoot tracks today?" asked Brian helpfully.

"I didn't, but that doesn't mean much. They are very stealthy. I mean, one could be out there, just beyond the firelight."

I stole a glance at the boys, who hung on every word. Soon Brian brought out his guitar and had everyone singing songs. This was my cue.

I made my escape with the costume unnoticed and found a hollow in the dense forest about one hundred yards from the campsite. Not too close but close enough to be well seen. I unfolded the suit.

It was show time!

The first problem was the fit. Why I hadn't bothered to try it on is anyone's guess (laziness?), but as I slid my legs into the bottom half, it became clear that it wasn't meant to be worn over clothes. I wasn't about to strip to my underwear in the evening chill, so I forced my legs inside till they looked like hirsute sausages. I then realized that

I needed a second person to Velcro closed the back. Finally, using a tree trunk to pin it and rolling my torso around, I got the dammed thing semiclosed.

I gave an Ohio Scream shriek. I could hear the campsite go deathly quiet. I grabbed the Bigfoot head, ready to put it on and step out into the trail where the boys would see me.

The second I put the head on I knew it was a disaster. The eyeholes were a good four inches too high. I could see nothing but black and could feel the rubber on my eyelashes. I was completely blind. No matter how I pulled and adjusted, I couldn't get the eyeholes to my eye level. But I had come too far; the stage was set, and there could be no turning back. With another shriek, I stepped out into the moonlit trail, caught my foot on a root and fell over headfirst.

"Mom, there's a dog lying down in the trail!" said one of the boys. (Although I couldn't see, I could hear perfectly.)

I was flooded with humiliated panic, convinced that imminently the boys would charge the "dog" to discover me in costume, flat on my face. There would be no way to explain it that wouldn't be the kind of mortifying scenario all parents desperately spend their lifetimes trying to avoid.

"Aaauuuughoooh!" I screamed, hoping to stave them off, as I crawled around on all fours, the tightness of the suit making it impossible to stand. "Aaauuuughooh!"

I made my way back into the thicket and out of eyeshot. By bearhugging a sequoia trunk I was eventually able to get to my feet. I was ready to try again.

I stepped back onto the trail. I tried to do the famous arm-swinging Bigfoot walk as best I could, considering I was trying not to fall over again. Now I heard the sounds of the kids freaking out.

"It's Bigfoot!"

"Oh my God!"

"Aaaah!"

There were excited—if petrified—squeals and then the unmistak-able sound of my nephew Jacob throwing up, which he did whenever he was scared. (Yet another thing I hadn't taken into consideration.) It began to dawn on me that maybe Sheryl had been right about this caper all along. But if I've learned anything in my decades as an actor, it is that if a performance is going into the weeds, you must commit even further. I assumed the body language of a "shocked" Sasquatch as best I could and grunted like a silverback.

The reaction from the campsite was exactly the clambering ruckus I had hoped for, save the vomiting. It was time to get offstage while the getting was good. Always leave them wanting more. But as I slowly attempted to get back to the forest, I heard the sounds of tiny feet run-ning my way. Within seconds whoever it was was right in front of me.

"Get out of here! You . . . you . . . *college student!*" said a voice I recognized as Matthew's. Then he kicked me in the nuts.

This time, my Ohio Scream was authentic. As I doubled over, I pulled the mask down to better see my attacker. Matthew stood before me defiantly. He wasn't going to let this hairy beast into his campsite. For all he knew, I *was* a college student, hopped up on God knows what, but he wasn't scared and was clearly taking no shit whatsoever.

I felt a mix of love and pride for him, quickly followed by the realization that somehow I had gotten myself into a predicament where I was being attacked by my seven-year-old son in the middle of the redwoods while dressed in an ill-fitting Bigfoot costume. After a brief stare-down, Matthew stalked proudly back to the campfire. I staggered into the woods clutching my groin, stumbling into a tent I hadn't previously noticed.

"What the hell?!" said an angry male voice from inside. "Who's out there?!" he demanded.

When I heard him fumbling with the tent's zipper, I tore the

Bigfoot head off and fled, crashing through brambles and chest-high ferns. I was positive I was going to be shot, and the circumstances of my death were certain to make me more famous than I ever was in life. But I was due for a lucky break and got one. No shots were fired, and the guy got frustrated by the tent zipper and gave up.

I got out of the costume, rolled it into a ball and ditched it for retrieval later. I wandered back into the campsite as if nothing had happened.

"Dad! Dad! Where were you?! We saw a Bigfoot!!" said the boys, who swarmed me, hopping into my arms and crawling all over me.

"C'mere, we'll show you where it was! Jacob got scared and vomited, and Matthew attacked it!" said my nephew Lucas, who was still breathing heavily.

"It was awesome!" said my smallest, Johnowen, with his mischievous smile.

"Is this true?" I asked Matthew, who, true to form, was standing coolly against a tree.

"I did what I had to do," he said evenly.

Brian and Jodi tried not to laugh, and Sheryl caught my eye and shook her head with a small smile. The boys chattered over each other the rest of the night, each trying to outdo the other in the retelling of their Bigfoot sighting. I just listened and nodded, drinking it in and hoping that I wouldn't be in too much pain the next day. When I tucked them into bed later, they still wanted to talk about their adventure.

They talk about it still. We all do. Our family has moved on to other adventures, first serious girlfriends, college, summer internships and more vacations, some very extravagant indeed. All provide ample memories. But not all of them will have staying power. Why do we remember some events and forget others, even ones that are truly extraordinary when they happen? I've thought about this a lot as my boys have grown into men, as I try to remember *everything* of our years together and yet can't. It seems to me that the big memories, the ones that become sacred, all have two things in common. First, they were *created*. They were moments that, as a family, we had a hand in making. And also, it seems that the strongest memories all have an element of pain or discomfort that is worked through somewhere along the way. Whether it's a kick in the groin in the redwoods or the melancholy of that first kindergarten drop-off, a memory's potency seems to have a direct correlation to the amount of conflicting emotions it contains.

So I tell my boys that they need to say yes to life, just do it, get out and make their own memories. I tell them to think of it as a vocation; after all, we never think twice about toiling for money and yet when our time comes it won't be our bank balance that comforts us. I tell them to not be afraid. Don't fear the rejection that can come from putting yourself out there. Don't avoid the boredom of the long road trip; the destination may surprise you and be worth every second. You will need something to talk about, something remembered. It might just make you interesting. It will certainly make you fulfilled. And by creating your own memories, you will always have something to share with the rest of us.

Johnowen, my nephew Lucas, Matthew and my nephew Jacob, stopping for directions as we search for Bigfoot.

No One Follows the Frog

In life we look to our parents to guide us, but we also need mentors, those voices that come without the baggage of being your blood. If we are lucky, we may run across someone who can fill in the blanks that our parents can't or won't, someone whose life experience is a shared and valuable gem. For me, that person was Bernie Brillstein.

Bernie was a large, white-bearded, loud, hilarious, opinionated, passionate connoisseur of all foods, in particular most restaurant bread baskets, and more significantly, one of the greatest and most accomplished talent managers Hollywood has ever known. He discovered Jim Henson and the Muppets. He managed most of the original cast of *Saturday Night Live*, including Gilda Radner, John Belushi, Chevy Chase and Dan Aykroyd. He also represented the man who discovered them all, Lorne Michaels. Bernie produced TV and movies and even ran a movie studio himself at one point. His projects included *Ghostbusters*, *Dangerous Liaisons*, *It's Garry Shandling's*

Show, ALF, Just Shoot Me!, The Sopranos and many others. He and his partner, Brad Grey, built the entertainment industry's most powerful management firm, whose clients included Brad Pitt, Nic Cage, Gwyneth Paltrow, Jennifer Aniston, Mike Myers, Dana Carvey, Zach Galifianakis, Courteney Cox, Orlando Bloom, Natalie Portman and many others, including me.

Bernie and Brad ran this empire with a stable of tough, smart managers, all of whom were renowned as iconoclasts and hilarious misfits. Their company was not cast with the cookie-cutter Armani-wearing drones of the big talent agencies. In fact, Bernie often wore a tracksuit to work before Carrie, his chic last wife, began insisting on a more upscale look. Bernie personally managed very few people. With so much on his plate (literally), he mainly managed those who had been there at the beginning. Henson and Belushi (until they died). Lorne Michaels, Ed O'Neill, Martin Short and one or two others.

In 1990 I hosted *SNL* for the first time. I loved Bernie the moment I met him; his was the loudest laugh during my monologue (I would later learn that that was part of his fiduciary duty). From that experience I became close to Lorne and then, through him, to Bernie. We would play doubles together, where Bernie would move surprisingly well—"like Gleason!" he would say—in spite of being close to 300 pounds. After a match one day, we had a long talk about life. He was funny and provocative, honest in a way that few are, particularly in show biz, and had a very realistic and specific idea of what I should be doing with my career. He was that rare man who, in his late fifties, was already a legend and needed no one, yet was still as excitable and engaged as a kid—he was still a lover and a dreamer. He loved talent, not "the deal" or "the press release" or the parlay into the Next Big Gig running an entertainment division for a conglomerate. He still, after all these years, loved artists. And he loved me. I asked him to be my manager and he said yes.

People who are not in show business ("civilians," as they are called by some) often ask: "What is the difference between an agent and a manager?" It's a good question. The most important distinction is that an agent must be licensed and can only charge you 10 percent. Truly anyone can be a manager and could charge as much as a client might pay. This is why you see so many sports figures with family members as managers bilking their clients into the poorhouse. Also, managers (in theory) used to do what agents traditionally didn't do. Managers planned long-term. They thought about "career planning," while the agent focused mostly on bringing any and every deal to the client.

But today, between superagent Mike Ovitz's eighties business influence and *Entourage*'s cultural one, agents have become stars. And as an actor, when your agent becomes a star, you'd better have someone keeping them honest. And so today, everyone has a manager.

Bernie loved keeping people honest. Which was pretty rare; the standard mode of honesty in Hollywood usually went something like this:

CLIENT

I'm really upset. The studio owes me money.

MANAGER OR AGENT

It's despicable . . . I'm gonna make a call and fix it!

CLIENT

Thanks. I just bought a new house and have another baby on the way.

ROB LOWE

MANAGER OR AGENT

I understand. How dare they! I'm gonna ream
these guys at [Paramount, Universal, NBC, HBO,
whatever].
I'll call you back!

CLIENT

Thanks, man.

MANAGER OR AGENT
(to his assistant)
Get me the head of [Paramount, Universal,
NBC, HBO, whatever].

The STUDIO or NETWORK PRESIDENT gets on the line.

PRESIDENT

Hello?

MANAGER

How dare my client cause you trouble like
this?!
I'm trying to talk sense into him.
Meanwhile, are you green-lighting the new
Channing Tatum movie?
Chan is very anxious to get started!

Bernie was different and everyone knew it. When I did a movie
that became a surprise hit and the studio tried to screw me, he called
the studio head with me sitting next to him. After a few pleasant-
ries the honcho told Bernie that "there was nothing [the studio] could

do" about the money owed me. Bernie erupted. "How 'bout go fuck yourself!" (This to one of the most revered, powerful and tenured studio heads in history.)

I had my money by the end of the week.

Bernie was by no means perfect. He often had truisms that I struggled to understand, among them: "Beware of redheaded Jews," and "Never trust people whose last names end in vowels." He assured me that I was exempt because "the 'e' in 'Lowe' is silent!"

Bernie and I spoke every day, multiple times. Any excuse was enough for us to talk. He was interested in and loved my family. He was Matthew's godfather. Sometimes we spoke for so long that it reminded me of the days of the never-ending teenage girlfriend telephone talks. Bernie guided me through many phases of life, marriage in particular. Never has better marital advice been dispensed by someone with so many wives.

His struggles with his weight were legend. "I've lost forty pounds!" he would say, yet look exactly the same. In the late nineties he and I were flying out of Aspen (a notoriously dangerous airport) on a private plane he had rented. We were with our wives, the comedy writer and *Breaking Bad* star Bob Odenkirk, David Spade and Hall of Fame TV producer George Schlatter, who also struggled with his weight.

"We have too much baggage, so I need to get a proper weight count," said the pilot sternly.

The wives answered, then me, then Odenkirk. I could see Bernie getting nervous.

"What about you, Mr. Brillstein?" asked the pilot.

"I weigh two hundred fifteen pounds," said Bernie with utter conviction.

Spade and I looked at each other disbelievingly.

"And you, Mr. Schlatter?"

"Two hundred five pounds!" he said.

Spade could take no more.

"Sir, I weigh two hundred eighty-five pounds," he volunteered. We took off safely.

It wouldn't be the last time Bernie's idiosyncrasies almost got me into hot water.

In spite of his love for sports, he always had terrible seats. When you would bust him on it, he would protest, "But I *like* my seats. They're near the exits!" Bernie also loved playing craps and Sheryl and I often went with him to Vegas, where he would bring fifty thousand dollars cash in a brown bag.

"I have great seats for the Holyfield fight," he told me on one such trip. He must've sensed my lack of enthusiasm because he added, "Don't worry, I spend so much at Bally's my host got 'em for us!"

Since I was a fight fan, Sheryl, Bernie and I went. It was Evander Holyfield vs. Mike Tyson. About as big a marquee fight as you could possibly want. The Strip was on fire that night, as it always is for the Big One, but that evening it was thick as a brick, even by Vegas standards. We knew we were in for an adventure but could not possibly have imagined what lay ahead.

In the VIP holding area of the MGM Grand we mingled with fellow actors, singers and star athletes. We chatted with Garry Shandling, Dennis Miller, Christian Slater and Nic Cage, until we were led en masse into the arena. I'm not too proud or blasé to deny that one of the better perks of success is the thrill of being led from the top of an arena all the way down to the front row. As we arrived ringside, Cage settled in next to Slater while Shandling and Miller tried to figure out who'd sit where. I'd been ringside before, a number of times, and seen Hagler, Tyson and others; I couldn't wait to see the sweat fly and feel the lovely violence, which is palpable at that range.

An usher looked at our tickets.

"Oh, right this way, Mr. Lowe," he said, and we followed him to the other side of the ring.

I waved over to the gang, who seemed confused that we weren't in the same area. I shrugged and pantomimed, "Let's meet up later," as Bernie, Sheryl and I fell in line again. This time the usher turned and began marching up the stairs and out of the VIP section.

It got ugly quickly.

Soon we were so high above the ring that I could barely make out the faces of my friends sitting ringside, although the look of horror on their faces as we were led to Siberia was something I was glad not to witness.

Like Sir Edmund Hillary summiting Everest without oxygen, our harrowing, debilitating ascent seemed to take forever. I'm certain Sheryl had never climbed higher in high heels. She might as well have been on a StairMaster.

Finally, mercifully, it was over.

"Here you are, Mr. Lowe," said the usher, who seemed to have the cardio capacity of Lance Armstrong on dope. "Enjoy the fight." Panting, I looked around. We were in the absolute top row of the arena. Bernie had struck again.

"Yo! Rob Lowe! Whatcha doin' up here!" shouted a large man with tattoos, wearing an oversized Oakland Raiders jersey.

"Just checkin' out the fight!" I smiled.

I helped Sheryl to her seat. She was being a champ, sucking it up and acting cool as a cucumber. Bernie, for his part, was silent and avoiding all eye contact, mopping the raining sweat off his brow.

"Hey! Hey! Excuse me! Hey! Yo!" yelled another guy holding a clown-sized cup of beer. "Hey, my wife says you're *somebody*! Are you *somebody*?!"

I tried to pretend I couldn't hear but my silence only emboldened him.

"Are you famous? She says you're famous! What do you play in?"

I wanted to tell him I didn't "play" in anything but had acted, directed, produced and written some things he might have seen.

"What do you *play* in? Can my wife kiss you?! She wants to kiss you!! I don't care, fuck it, it's Vegas, right?! What do you play in?!"

This kind of patter happens more than you might think, and I've come to accept it as the cost of doing business. I also knew that it was likely to continue unless something more interesting got the couple's attention.

Happily, in the third round, Mike Tyson had one of the greatest meltdowns in the history of all sports and bit off Evander Holyfield's right ear. This shut the guy up. Finally.

The entire arena was on its feet. No one knew what to think. Was the fight over? What was going on in that ring? God knows from our seats we could barely tell it was a boxing match at all. When the referee disqualified Iron Mike and ended the fight, the crowd's mood turned ugly. Like a switch being thrown, the place felt very unsafe. Bernie, always a pro at reading a room, whispered to me urgently.

"Let's get the fuck out of here, kid."

Taking direction is what I do for a living, so I grabbed Sheryl and hightailed it. For once, I was happy to be so close to the exits.

The doors to the arena had barely slammed behind us when the crowd went absolutely bat-shit. I could hear yelling and the unmistakable rumblings of an angry mob. Quickly, we made our way from the MGM sports complex into the casino, where we caught our breath. Soon, surly, wild-eyed fight patrons began filling in around us.

"I'll see you kids at brunch, I'm going up," said Bernie wisely.

"Sheryl and I are gonna gamble," I said stupidly.

My wife loves her some casino. She is completely capable of sitting uninterrupted for eight or nine hours in front of a slot machine. She strokes it, talks to it and gazes upon it with a face that is usually reserved only for the handsome werewolf guy on *True Blood*. Since I am not single, don't drink and hate gambling, for me Vegas always becomes a lonely adventure in room service and ESPN. For me, "what happens in Vegas" is . . . not much.

But not tonight.

In the time it took Bernie to walk to the elevators, the entire casino floor had been transformed into a sea of fight fans bent on destruction. Packs of scary-looking dudes eyeballed anyone who glanced their way. The area was thick with people. If there was such a thing as maximum capacity, the casino was now very close to it, and suddenly it was very hard to move.

Sheryl and I exchanged glances. It was a very bad crowd; we were packed among them like sardines and it was time to get out.

Then came the unmistakable sound of gunshots.

Pop. Pop. Pop. In rapid succession. The triple burst that is the proper way to shoot a semiautomatic handgun. Between recreational shooting in my civilian life and working with all kinds of weapons over the years on sets, I knew what I heard. Someone in the crowd was a shooter.

In the panic that exploded, men were throwing their wives under tables, screams rang out and people began to scramble in confusion, pushing and knocking over anything in their way. I grabbed Sheryl by the arm, hard. Her eyes were huge and scared.

"Follow me!" I shouted.

I put her behind me, lowered my shoulder and began to jog through the panicked and roiling crowd. I watched as a gang of young men overturned a blackjack table. I saw people grabbing and pocketing the chips that flew everywhere.

This escalated things quickly. Now the security staff began wading in, meaning business, and from the looks on everyone's faces on both sides of the equation, I knew people were about to be badly hurt.

There was a single, piercing woman's scream followed by aggressive male yelling. I could see a crowd of probably a hundred people start to run from whatever was going down. Within a second it was a stampede in the casino.

I threw Sheryl around a corner as the mass ran past us. We found ourselves at the top of a long, thin hallway leading to a single half-open door.

"C'mon!" I said, heading down the hall, but it was too late; behind us people, running at top speed and frantic, began to fill in the hallway, packing at our backs, pressing on us, ready to trample us. More rushed in behind them. A security guard appeared from the other side of the semiopen door, saw the stampede coming his way and panicked. He fumbled to kick open the doorstop in an effort to close it.

I knew that if he was able to close the door in front of us, Sheryl and I would be crushed. Together, we ran as fast as we could. The guard had released the stopper and was beginning to slam it shut. He was standing in the remaining space between the door and the jamb as I lowered my shoulder and speared him, lifting him off his feet. Sheryl and I blew past him as he lay on the ground gathering himself. We kept running and I never turned back.

Eventually, we made our way to a friend's room to wait out the chaos, which had now spilled into the streets. Looking out the window, I saw a man lying motionless on the concrete below. I couldn't tell his condition but he was alone, lying facedown in an awkward position, unmoving.

After a few hours the sirens began to quiet and I began to feel it might be safe to venture outside. I thanked my pal for the safe haven and called to Sheryl, who was gazing out at the street. I went to her and put my arms around her.

"I think we can go home now," I said.

She nodded and I could tell she was still a little scared. Below us, the man still lay motionless, alone and forgotten. I never found out what became of him.

Clearly Las Vegas is light-years from the days of the mob and its lawless history. In fact, there is probably not a more closely regulated or corporate destination in the world (which is why its over-the-top sales pitch of Krazy Debauchery for the Masses makes me chuckle). But when the next day's paper carried only an innocuous blurb about "champagne corks popping" and "confusion" in the casino, I knew that Sin City was still a company town. Zero mention of the riot, the stampede, the gaming tables being overturned, the missing chips or the man lying on the concrete. Apparently, the town's motto is true. Vegas can truly still keep a secret.

I vowed to never attend a sporting event with Bernie ever again. But we continued our daily talks filled with the discussion of the details of life: kids, finances, career planning, gossip and anything and everything that might be of interest.

In the summer of 2008, after a number of years of health struggles, Bernie was rushed to a hospital in Los Angeles. Although his family and many friends hoped for another recovery, another crash diet or new fitness program, there was a sense that Bernie, despite his will and strength, had reached his limit.

Bernie was in the ICU for weeks. He barred all visitors. Sheryl and I of course were having none of it. We crashed our way into his room whenever we could. By this point, one of the greatest storytellers I have ever known was communicating via handheld chalkboard. Although he was fighting for his life, all he wanted to talk about was mine.

He was half-asleep as we entered but gamely tried to rally at the sound of my voice. Soon he was asking questions. "*Brothers & Sisters?*" he scrawled, referring to the show I was currently doing.

"New deal at ABC!" he wrote, underlining it, and I could see in his eyes his desire for one more killing, one more big win for his client.

I held his hand. Sheryl fixed his hair. He was happy to see us but embarrassed to be seen as he was. We entertained him with stories of the things he loved. The LA Kings, the Hollywood industry inside scoop, redheaded Jews and people whose names ended in vowels. When it was time for us to go he threw down his chalkboard and raised himself up to speak, but I couldn't make out what he wanted to say. As he lay back down he had tears streaming down his face. And I knew him so well that I understood at once the gesture that followed, which meant: "Isn't this just such *bullshit*, kid?!"

Standing behind him, Sheryl, who had always been mad for him, was silently weeping. I shot her a look: "Don't let him see you like that."

We both hugged him good-bye and I'm sure we all knew it was the real thing. I kissed his head, looked into his eyes and told him I'd be by the next day right after I was done shooting.

I didn't cry until I got into the hallway.

I was sitting next to Calista Flockhart, among a crew of seventy-five, preparing for my close-up on set in a hospital ICU when my phone rang. I knew before I answered. Bernie was gone. I hung up in a daze and the cameras were already rolling. Calista held my hand. An actor playing an ICU nurse was reading her lines: "Congratulations! You are having a baby boy!" The camera began to push in, till it was inches from my face, until my eyes lost focus as I tried to stop them from filling with tears.

"Aaaaaaand cut! Let's print that and move on," said the director. And so we did, because that's how it is.

When you live as large as Bernie Brillstein, when you are as revered and loved and have influenced so many, you better secure a very big venue for the memorial service. With the exception of Lew Wasserman's memorial, there hadn't been a turnout like there was for Bernie in decades, and so the service at Royce Hall at UCLA was standing-room only on a beautiful day in mid-August.

Bernie, who absolutely hated poorly run events and had even less patience for dull ones, would have been apoplectic with agita. He also would've been literally sweating the guest list ("Why is *that* fucker here?" or "How great is Jen Aniston?!"). Luckily for Bernie, two of his great collaborators were in charge of the giant memorial: his former partner and now president of Paramount Pictures, Brad Grey, and Lorne Michaels. It was a perfect match. Brad kept everyone in line, made things happen, and Lorne produced it down to the smallest grace note. When it was over, it would go down in Hollywood history as one of the most memorable and moving tributes. (Although it was a great movie and became a hit, *Tropic Thunder* had the misfortune of premiering at the same time, ten blocks away, to a deserted red carpet. Everyone was at Bernie's send-off.)

There was not an agent, manager or television or movie executive who wasn't there. There were the figures who knew the quiet, personal part of Bernie. The lover, who had time for almost everyone he met, the dreamer who saw an entire career just by looking into an artist's face. And people like his favorite waitress at Nate 'n Al's deli, who had served him for thirty years and whose child's school tuition Bernie had helped fund. There are 1,834 seats in Royce Hall; that day every single one was taken, and many more stood.

Backstage, the alphas were in full but respectful peacock mode. The list of eulogists was a roster of comedy killers like Martin Short, Bill Maher, David Spade, Jon Lovitz and old-guard assassins like Norm Crosby and Jack Burns. Megaproducer Jerry Weintraub, *SNL* writer Alan Zweibel, both Brad and Lorne, Jennifer Aniston and I would also speak. There would be Dan Aykroyd and Jim Belushi performing as the Blues Brothers, as well as Kermit the Frog.

Everyone had two goals: remembering their fallen father and absolutely *killing* it in front of all of Hollywood. After all, this was mainly a comedy crowd, and if you don't think there's no one more competitive than a big-time pro comic, then you've never met one.

"Looorne," crooned Jon Lovitz in his distinctive tone, "when do I speak?"

"I'm doing the order now," said Lorne in the same focused/casual manner in which he runs *SNL*.

"I think the Blues Brothers should open," suggested Jerry Weintraub helpfully.

"I'm keeping it short," said Brad Grey.

"Try to be funny, Jon," said Spade to his old *SNL* pal.

"Kermit or Blues Brothers first?" asked a production assistant with a clipboard.

"Can I see the running order?" asked Brad Grey.

"Put me with Jennifer Aniston!" said Lovitz.

"Just tell me who's gonna close the show, okay?!" someone demanded.

Lorne had had enough.

"I haven't finished the speaking order, but I will tell you this: No one follows the frog."

When we did speak, the order, like everything that evening, was perfect. Everyone spoke deeply of their love for Bernie and lampooned him with equal measure. He would have *loved* it. There were times when I knew exactly when I would have heard his booming laugh/yell: "AAAAH HAAAAH!"

When we were all done, and after John's brother Jim partnered with Dan on the Blues Brothers hit "Soul Man," I remembered something Bernie always said about one of his most famous and tragically lost clients.

"Kid, I'm pretty sure there's no heaven. If there was, Belushi would have called."

I thought of them both, now reunited, probably looking down at us, laughing, wearing comfy tracksuits, as Bernie's discovery Kermit the Frog appeared onstage. Sitting on a log, he began to sing. I recognized the song at once, as did many around me in the audience, and you could plainly hear stifled gasps and muffled sobbing.

I remembered the last time I saw Bernie and how he tried to speak but I couldn't hear him. I thought of his joke about not hearing from Belushi from heaven. I thought about how lucky I was to have known him and how much I would miss him, as Kermit sang "Rainbow Connection":

Have you been half-asleep and have you heard voices?
I've heard them calling my name.
Is this the sweet sound that called the young sailors?
The voice might be one and the same.
I've heard it too many times to ignore it
It's something that I'm supposed to be.
Someday we'll find it, the rainbow connection
The lovers, the dreamers and me.

Sheryl and I with the irreplaceable Bernie Brillstein.

No Comparison

When I was young and wild, being a father was the farthest thing from my mind. The only extent to which it was ever a consideration was the lengths I went to in order to avoid becoming one. I would see parents with their kids, chasing them around malls or shushing them in restaurants, and think, "What a nightmare." Having children seemed exhausting and life with them boring. And in my twenties, nothing was more repellent than being boring.

But my dark secret was that I connected to kids. I related to them, even as an "it-boy/man" eighties media sensation. In truth, some of the more grounded and humane times I can recall from that crazy era were moments when I would find myself confronted with, say, a friend's newborn or when I was commandeered into spending time with kids.

In a decade where there is so much I don't remember, I think it's significant that these moments stay with me, even today. Clearly, even though I didn't know it at the time, the relationship between fathers and children spoke to me.

When I changed my life, when I sobered up, when I saw that show business couldn't fill that place that was empty, those buried feelings rose, and having found the love of the right woman, I started a family of my own. The best chapter of my life began.

Together, the four of us left Los Angeles to make a stab at a normal life, to the extent that someone like me can ever have one. We found a town where not everyone on the PTA was a studio executive or agent or absent on location with their latest project. Not that there is anything wrong with that, but since I had the ability to live outside Hollywood, I wanted my boys to have a more diverse social environment, because LA truly is a company town. And, so, instead they were raised with kids whose parents were from all walks of life, and today I see the dividends in my boys' broad spectrum of interests. And, so far, neither has asked me to get him a SAG card.

As a child of divorce (three of them, if you are keeping score at home), my experience with fathering was limited. Although I am blessed to have a loving relationship with my dad, he was gone from my daily life (other than summers) once I was four years old. Then there were two stepfathers, the first also a good man and the second a man of complex inconsistencies. Like so many, I never had a consistent male figure who wasn't eventually switched out.

So, when my time came, I took the many good things I learned from the men in my life and was left to make up the rest from whole cloth.

Being a father became the focus of my life. My career was now a means to an end, to make it easier to devote myself to my real passion: helping Sheryl raise our boys. I still worked with drive and purpose. I think some of my best work was done in this period, this era where

I had the perspective to know that a hit movie or TV show is great, but your sons growing up healthy and well-rounded is better.

It's funny how almost all clichés turn out to be dead on the money. It's not a new concept, but I am constantly amazed by how much a young man needs both his mother and father. At the same time. In the same debates. Giving equal push-back and support. I hate to think of the mess I would have made raising Matthew and Johnowen without Sheryl's 24/7 presence. And vice versa (although she'd probably have done better without me than the other way around). I need her unrelenting attention to detail, her indefatigable drive for organization and order, and most of all, her utterly selfless ability to put her needs last as she focuses like a laser on the needs and wants of those she loves. She hooked a complicated fish with me, and I can't see another being able to love me and our boys with her nuclear devotion.

My strengths lie elsewhere. I am, to put it mildly, not detail-oriented and not particularly orderly. I *do* like those around me to be, however. I, like many in my line of work, can fall easily into self-centeredness, which is probably the single worst noncriminal attribute a parent can have. There is no greater curse than being the child of a narcissist. Not that I'm copping to being a narcissist, mind you. I'd like to think I have a modicum of self-awareness that allows me to avoid at least the clinical diagnosis (although the brilliant and astute Rashida Jones claims that I am what she likes to call a *benevolent* narcissist). I'm well suited to run interference with teachers, parents, administrators, friends of my boys or any other third parties who inevitably enter the family equation. I am happy to engage, argue, charm or advocate as needed. I'm the "face" guy for our family, while Sheryl works her magic behind the scenes. Different people, different skills, but both needed.

Soon we will have to find another use for those skills. For a brief time your children belong to you, but soon they belong to the world. I am humbled to watch this process play out in my life as my little boys begin to go their own way. It makes me proud and it breaks my heart. And so, now, like any unadmitted but possibly qualified benevolent narcissist would say, "What about *me?*"

I suppose I could buy a Harley or a seventies muscle car and drive along the coast with Sheryl until we sit side by side holding hands in matching claw-footed tubs placed strategically on a beautiful ocean-front cliff, like in those erectile dysfunction commercials. I could adopt a litter of puppies. I could dust off the old golf clubs, the ones I hung up when the boys were born, despite having killed the Iowa state bird in flight with a wedge shot the last time I played. I could write another book, I guess. I could do a lot of things with the new expanse of free time I will have. But first I will have to come to see it as an opportunity and not as a loss. I know I'll get there soon; I'm not there yet. But I'm trying. We are the authors of our own lives; it falls only to us. It's time for me to pick up that pen and begin to write again. Because my hope is that the story of my life with Sheryl has many chapters. I'm blessed to have finished such a beautiful one.

People sometimes ask me if I have any advice for how to maintain a long and successful marriage, having been happily married for more than twenty-two years.

I used to wonder the same thing when I looked from afar at my hero, Paul Newman, and observed his longtime union with Joanne Woodward. They were always Hollywood's happy example, the exception to the cliché of ridiculous and frivolous show-biz marriages.

And while it's true that Newman's love affair is to be admired, I disagree with the notion that the entertainment business has a lower success rate at marriage than any other high-stress, high-stakes line of work. I'm sure it's just as hard for couples in the military or others who are forced to spend weeks or months apart in the forced company of many new personalities, some of whom can be quite compelling, charming and attractive. In the end, in terms of temptation and loneliness, there's probably not much difference between being on a movie location in Saskatoon for four months or being on an oil rig in the North Sea for the same amount of time.

I suppose the idea that Hollywood is the center of kooky love affairs isn't helped by reality stars who marry for publicity or the number of truly certified wackos who have every right to give love a shot, but after a year or so have only a tattoo of their partner to show for it. But my judgment is that kind of thing happens everywhere, all the time. You just hear about it more in my business because people are paying attention.

Regardless of your circumstances, the best bet you have for long-term marriage is obvious: Choose well. Many don't. They do it for the great sex or the life they hope to achieve with their partner or with the thinking that with the commitment of marriage things will be simpler and better. Some do it because they really want to get married, instead of really wanting to *be* married. Many don't know the difference.

I was not looking to get married. If you weren't aware of me in the eighties, let me just say that I was quite active in the R and D arena of female companionship. In fact, when I first met Sheryl I was still in the thick of being a single, twentysomething male movie star maniac.

Even then, Sheryl cut through the clutter. Physically, she was stunning. And please, people, let's drop all the highfalutin PC pretense here; someone's looks are important. They are the first thing we judge each other on, and it's impossible not to; we can't "know" anyone from across a crowded room. And when I saw this tall, long-legged blonde with her particularly emotive sky-blue eyes, I wanted to know her.

It was a double date, a blind one; we had been set up by a friend, and I am forever in his debt. But I'm sure that he could never have imagined that margaritas and chips at a Mexican restaurant would lead to my life today, and looking back these twenty-two years, the fact that it was a blind date seems all the more incredible.

That I had no preview of how I might feel about Sheryl makes the fact that I came to love her a true odds-defier. But consider Sheryl's situation: She *knows* she's meeting me. Seen a movie or two, read the *National Enquirer*. Probably heard some opinions about me, possibly from many and probably for quite a while. I was used to everyone having a preconceived notion of who I was.

Sheryl didn't.

She saw parts of me no one had before. She somehow knew I longed to be better than I was. She saw potential in me to be more, as an actor and as a man. As we got to know each other, she emboldened me to do things that I hadn't dared before. To quit drinking. To get sober. To try to stop chasing the latest, hottest girl. I began to grow.

When she would visit my *Miami Vice*–looking Hollywood Hills bachelor pad, she would decorate. I have a vivid memory of her reorganizing the books and items on my coffee table into a design straight out of Ralph Lauren. She would also often insist we stock my kitchen with more than a beer bong and Wolfgang Puck's frozen pizzas. Then she would cook her special pasta broccoli. While these are not revolutionary efforts, for me they might as well have been. No one had ever thought to do any of it for me before.

Somehow I had the courage and the foresight to ask her to marry me, and in the most fortunate moment I will surely ever have, she said yes. I had come to see that Sheryl would jump in front of a train for me (I am not speaking metaphorically) *and* that I was never likely to find her mix of passion, beauty, sexuality, friendship and unconditional love in anyone else.

I feel that way still. In sobriety, one learns that all anyone has is today. Yesterday cannot be relived. Tomorrow is guaranteed to no one. For me, this is the key to every facet of my life. I try (and sometimes fail) to keep it simple and just do the next right thing. It is a very easy concept but sometimes very hard to do. I haven't always done it, but I will never stop trying. Sheryl demands only progress, not perfection. She loves me in spite of my flaws.

I also love her for her shortcomings. When you can love those, and not be resentful or hope they will magically disappear, you are approaching unconditional love. And like any partner who consciously takes stock of their union, Sheryl works hard to grow and better herself.

It's easy to lose track of your love affair when the children come. It's happened to us. It's hard not to put all your emotional time into the very embodiment of your shared love. After a long day at work, it was sometimes easier to hop in bed with the kids, read Harry Potter and fall asleep with them than do the late-night catch-up of the daily minutiae of running a house, businesses and marriage. But the kids will be only as happy as their parents, which is something to be remembered in our age of total emotional focus on our children. I have had that concept underlined for me recently as our boys prepare to move out and Sheryl and I will once again have each other with nothing to distract us.

Intimacy does not come to me easily. I am finding, as I continue to try to understand myself, that deep talks do not mean deep relationships, and that in spite of my chronological age, I still have barriers, probably from childhood, that sometimes keep me distant on the inside, although you wouldn't see it on the outside. Unless, of course, you know me well. I don't want to be one of those nice guys who people like well enough, I guess, but don't have a deep connection to. I want to be *known*. I want to be seen for all I am, not just what you see on the surface. But it is up to me to let you in, to give you the keys to know me in that way, and to do the work of connecting beyond what is comfortable and easy.

I say this because at twenty-two years into my marriage I have realized that I want to love Sheryl better. I want to refocus on the one thing that has made the most positive impact on my life and changed me beyond my ability to articulate: my love for her.

I was taught to people-please; Sheryl showed me how to fight for myself. I was an equal-opportunity companion; Sheryl taught me social discretion. I am still a procrastinator in key areas; Sheryl is an example of industrious immediacy. She has a keen and quick instinct for people and events; I am slower on the uptake, too often willing to give the benefit of the doubt.

She has also taught me, through the long parade of days and nights, through our valleys and all the way up to our euphoric altitudes, that I am worthy of her love. I know I can fail and she will love me. I know I can fall and she will love me and I also know that I will rarely do either with her as my muse, my partner, my lover. She has seen through the veneer that I want everyone to see, the persona I have been fashioning since almost as long as I can remember, to the complicated rough part I hide and often deny I have.

I want our next chapter to be deeper. And that means digging, and digging is hard, exhausting work. But a recommitment seems important now; maybe it's moving through the two-decade anniversary, maybe it's my age. But whatever the reason, I know I want it because my original commitment to that younger version of Sheryl led to a life of bounty I could never have imagined.

I am not a very superstitious person. Although I do have some superstitions: I won't mention *Macbeth* in a theater (or whistle) and won't walk under ladders. I am also against tempting fate by talking too much of my good fortune in having found Sheryl. No one likes a jinx. But people *do* ask me how (and why) I embraced marriage, because clearly, I could've been a great wingman for George Clooney or my old pal Charlie Sheen (who needs no wingman; he is his own air force).

Everyone who is married, wants to be married or was married is interested in someone else's marriage. It's how we judge our own relationships. It is to what we compare our own story. So I understand why people want to know what I've learned about long-term love, just as I wondered about Paul Newman's marriage. And this, simply, is all I know: Everyone's love is different. My marriage is not like my parents' or Sheryl's parents', it's not like my brother's or my best friend's and it's not like yours. In spite of our wanting to, we cannot compare. Our successes and failures in love are unique to us alone. And in the end, that's because our partners are as one-of-a-kind as we are. I know mine is. She is blond, five feet eight, with blue eyes. She has a widow's peak and the long legs of a teenager. She has a huge heart. She reads slowly. She is a math genius and often does not find me funny. She is loyal to the last stand and quick to defend. She is a mother to all who need it and to many who don't. She gives great toasts and is a better public speaker and writer than she will ever know. She is a wellspring of creativity and a lover of bad television. She single-handedly keeps afloat the company that manufactures Swedish Fish, as well as Costco. She has too many Hermès bags and works too hard to pay for them. She has created two success-ful companies, had at least three different careers and raised two world-class young men. She took a man-child and turned him into a man. She made me what I am today. There will never be another like her and our love, like everyone's, has no answers and no comparisons.

Sheryl and I falling in love
on location in Israel, 1990.

Love on the red carpet.

New Year's Eve photo
booth fun.

Love Life

Overthinking, while not as egregious a flaw as, say, lying or murder, is nonetheless a dubious luxury of those with too much time to do it and can stall or force us into some very difficult circumstances in life. Fear of the Wrong Choice has paralyzed many a man from saying yes to the right woman (and vice versa), stopped us from quitting jobs that hold us back, from having the loves of our lives until we're absolutely *sure* we're "ready to have children," from leaving relationships we need to, and kept us on the wrong side of many other life barriers too numerous to name here. We weigh and we question, we work the angles and list the pros and cons, while we move one step up and two back toward actually taking action. We delude ourselves that we are doing our due diligence when mostly we are just treading water in a perfectly heated pool of laziness, comfort and fear. You can't study the map forever. At some point it's time to start walking; there is only so much daylight.

I've been overthinking this last chapter of the book. Like some

Oscar winners I know who agonize over their follow-up work, I've gotten precious about writing in the shadow of my first book, wanting the same positive reaction but not wanting to chase it, wanting this one to be better in every way but not wanting to force it. And now, here at the end, I've gotten a little tight. I want to go out with a bang; I want to make it count.

I feel fairly sheepish about this overthinking but after twenty-three years of sobriety, I've learned that when you are stuck, the best thing you can do is to start walking. I pick up my pen; let's get on with this.

And just like that, as I've experienced and observed in my decades in recovery, my *willingness* opens the door to inspiration. Just now, buckled into seat 3A of Delta's flight 2040 to JFK, I've been given the gift of something I need to write about. Because sitting here with my cheap Bic pen and legal pad, next to a sleeping businessman, something incredible has happened, and I have a confession to make.

I am no longer sober.

For the first time in almost as long as I can remember, I have taken a drink. I can feel the alcohol igniting through my veins, making my head feel like a sparkler waved on a summer night and tasting like gasoline. My adrenaline is up and my heart is pumping. I'm filled with both shame and euphoria. I've had only the first sip, but already my thoughts fly to the possibilities now awaiting me. I see escape, adventure, dark and daring subterranean sojourns that I wonder if I can still navigate. Or want to. I think of my wife and my sons. Sheryl, who inspired me to get sober, and Matthew and Johnowen, who have never known me not so. It has the exhilaration of rebirth, this first taste, but it also feels like death, foreboding and heavy with the dark and visceral sickly sweetness, that certain precursor to all things that end badly.

I look around the plane's cabin to see if anyone is paying attention to me as I hold the drink. They aren't. But the woman on her iPad is reading TMZ and the headline is "Star of *Glee* Found Dead in Vancouver Hotel at 31, Had Battled Addiction in Past."

As I would have prayed for, I want this opportunity, this fork in the road, to be over. No one would ever be the wiser; it could be my little secret, but I'm thankfully, gratefully, not having it.

"Excuse me." I signal the flight attendant. "I asked for an orange juice and you gave me a mimosa."

Although I was trying to be as blasé as I could stand, he must have picked up on something, and I watch his face visibly pale.

"Oh. Oh! I'm *so* sorry! I . . . I . . . mixed up the order!" he stammers.

I hand him the mimosa, one sip missing from its full content.

"I can't believe I did that! Here, let me get you your orange juice," he says as he flees to the galley.

This honest mistake, this bizarre mix-up, has taken about five seconds. Long enough for me to get my unexpected and unwanted dose of Delta's finest champagne and long enough to see my life flash before my eyes. I'm glad that I don't have to start over in recovery as a newcomer, giving up my twenty-three years to start at day one. I remember the panic I felt years ago — maybe I was six months sober — when I reached for my Perrier and lime and took my tablemate's gin and tonic by mistake.

"If it's an accident and it's only one sip, don't count it," people who knew better told me. Clearly, I am more even-keeled since that early switch-up, as I didn't spray this first sip on a sleeping businessman, like the spit take I performed as a newbie.

Soon both my heart rate and the flustered flight attendant have calmed down. I'm glad I can see the humor in the midair mix-up. I'm glad I had a full pen and a blank pad handy to write about the incident. And I'm reminded that one of the things I love most about life is its surprising way of suddenly placing you in its exciting and mysterious narrative.

————

My love life began probably earlier than it should have, although it didn't seem particularly so at the time. But one of the gifts of having children is that they offer the ability to see your long-gone young self as you look upon them. And when I think of my boys in the first grade I know that is not the ideal age to be coerced into an ad-hoc gyne-cological exam by a third-grade Lolita in her backyard pup tent. In the stifling, musty and mildewed Salvation Army bivouac, the pretty blonde shocked into life what would become a pattern throughout mine: the excitement and buzz of the unexpected romantic rendez-vous. This pattern was only reinforced by another, older neighbor-hood towhead who engineered the loss of my virginity by a sneak attack disguised as a home-cooked dinner when her parents were away. With her birthday gift of a condom, she had, with an admirable lack of subtlety, set the evening's agenda. And like any red-blooded teen, I took my cue and ran with it.

Soon, I would get my sea legs and begin to hone the skills all young men need to hunt for love (and sex) in the great big world. And over time I developed a fairly competent facility. But those first two sexual experiences had two consequences that would both help and harm me as the years unfolded.

When I became a famous teenager, I was already familiar with what it was like to be sought out for the purpose of romance, sex or fantasy. And for those of you who have not been a teen idol, let me assure you that 90 percent of the female fans have almost zero interest in your songs, movies, TV shows, what have you. It is almost exclusively about finding a receptacle for their exploding female sexuality. You are not particularly special, you just happen to be standing in the right place at their right time. When Justin Bieber accepts an MTV Video Music Award (or whatever) and begs to be "taken seriously as an artist," it is likely because he suspects Biebermania has very little to do with Bieber the artist. And from my experience, he would be correct.

I had learned from the pup tent and the condom birthday gift to sit back and enjoy it. And while it was a great run from my teens into my twenties and I enjoyed every minute of my time as a young, famous actor, it was too overwhelming, too intense, too *fun* for me to learn anything about what real love was or to notice that I was mostly immune to, and incapable of, intimacy. I was too young to know that I was squandering/being robbed of the very years when most young men are developing their empathy, vulnerability, honesty and compassion to share with their partner. I had those qualities as an actor because to excel, I had to, but personally I did not, because I didn't have to, and frankly, it would have been wasted in the world I found myself in.

Sure, I had relationships, and a number of them were deep and important to me. But even so, I was never really in with both feet. The temptations and situations that present themselves daily to a teen movie star proved too irresistible for me to experience the daily lessons that your first serious relationships should teach you. Jealousy, boredom, commitment, honesty, vulnerability and all the other often-times-uncomfortable feelings that come with truly being present for your romantic partner, I was able to disassociate from. If I felt any sort of malaise, instead of learning that all feelings (even bad ones) pass if given time, I made myself feel better by sampling the sexual circus that was always waiting just outside my door. My growing affinity for alcohol only made it easier. It quieted any conscience I might've had about bailing on a relationship under the cover of darkness for the Next Big Thing.

Somewhere, sometime in the mideighties, someone invited me to see the Hot New Act at the Universal Amphitheatre. The show was the talk of LA, sold out and *the* place to be. The new artist was unlike anything anyone had seen before: provocative, in-your-face sexual and suddenly inescapable on the radio. She was cute and she was young and she was single, and so I sat front-row to check out Madonna.

Although my tastes in those days ran more to Springsteen, the Stones and Tom Petty, her wedding gown/virgin shtick had the desired effect. One of the things I love about life is seeing an artist coming into their moment; this was Madonna's. That night she was a revelation.

"Madonna would like to see you backstage," a security guard said as the house lights came up.

"Sure!" I answered, although I was surprised she knew I was at the show. In those days, despite starring in movies, I was always shocked that anyone made a fuss over me.

I was taken to her dressing room. I expected it to be packed with the LA scenesters, but it was just me, some folks from her tour and a rep from the record company.

Madonna entered wearing a white cotton robe.

"Hiiii! Nice to meet you. So glad you came!"

She had flawless skin and eyes that imparted secrets from the moment you saw them.

We talked about her show; she asked what movie I was working on and so I told her a little about *St. Elmo's Fire*, which I had just finished.

"I play the bad boy," I said.

Madonna just smiled. She seemed to like that.

It was a crazy time in my life, and she was also just exploding. We kept in touch and ran into each other once or twice, but there was never any time where there weren't people around us, so it never really went anywhere.

We made a date to meet up in New York City. She was doing a concert and I was shooting the *Rolling Stone* cover for *St. Elmo's*. I was under no illusion that with our insane lives there would ever be room for much of a relationship, but at least some fun was clearly in the offing.

After my photo shoot I went to meet her at the Palladium, a giant dance club that was filled with rabid "boy-toy" doppelgänger fans of both sexes. It was a madhouse. I could feel our fledgling "date" going awry from the beginning. As I tried to enter the club, someone noticed me, word spread and things got unruly. There was a lot of grabbing and pawing. (This kind of thing never happens today, because most fans need both hands to hold their iPhones while they film you.) Club security grabbed me and bum-rushed me inside.

"Madonna's waiting for you. Follow me."

We headed to the VIP area. I saw Madonna holding court behind the velvet rope, with a great-looking dude sitting next to her, chatting her up. She looked up, saw me, smiled and waved me over. She motioned to have Mr. Good-Looking removed. Midrap he was yanked away, making room for me. I was impressed with her brazen matter-of-factness, as well as her command of logistics.

We talked for a while but the music was pounding. The DJ was playing "Holiday" and "Material Girl" at levels that could've split the atom. From our perch above the dance floor we could see it packed, wall to wall, with people hot and sweating and going berserk to the music of their new icon.

Madonna and I were discussing where we would sneak off to at the end of the evening when she suddenly jumped up and said, "Let's dance!"

"Out *there*?" I asked. After my chaotic entrance to the club I couldn't fathom what would happen to us on the dance floor, while they played her music.

"Yes, 'out there'!" she said teasingly, and the question was clear: Was I man enough to do it? But it seemed way over the top.

"I'll wait here," I said.

"Suit yourself," she replied as she waded beyond the velvet rope into the fray.

"You're crazy!" I said, half meaning it.

"No. I'm not," she said, stopping and looking directly into my eyes. "I'm just not going to let success fuck up my fun." She turned and disappeared into her fans.

The next time I saw her was twenty years later at a premiere in London: we both had our kids with us and they were about the same age. We were both happily married. We laughed about how long it had been. There was no need to even acknowledge how much had happened to both of us since those days of "Like a Virgin" and *St. El-mo's Fire*. She was still an icon, a trendsetter, and I admired that she had lived many chapters, writ large, and was better for it. Many had come and gone, blatantly co-opting her style, but she was still there, as interesting as ever.

Sometimes what I love most about life is its unpredictability and how, over time, the truth is revealed. "Like a Virgin" was not a "one-off" from a one-hit-wonder bimbo. Our Palladium sure thing was not meant to be (and it's a much more interesting story for it) and I never would've thought that I would look back on that night for the reason that I do.

"I won't let success fuck up my fun" seems profound to me now.

It makes me reflect on what the definition of "fun" is. I know it has been different things to me in different phases of my life. Back in Dayton, Ohio, it was children's theater and throwing snowballs at the city bus. In midseventies Malibu, it was going on auditions and attempting to get girls. In the eighties Brat Pack days it was making movies and *getting* girls. In the nineties it was attempting to find my authentic self and finding the right woman to love me and give me amazing babies. The new century brought a resurgent career and the adventure of raising a family. Today I'm finding that fun is to be found in embracing that I am once again in transition. Both boys are almost out of the house, and I have finished a long run on *Parks and Recreation*. I have no idea what the future holds professionally. I will develop my own TV show; I have some interesting ideas, but you never know what will work.

But I do know this. I have a great life partner in Sheryl, and whatever happens as I move forward, it will be fun. And as Madonna said, "I won't let success fuck up my fun," because I put less and less value on success. It's the process that counts. It's the people I get to connect with, most of whom will never be famous or want to be. It's the *intention* that gives the action value, not the results. Most actors (and many people) start out to please others. The trick is to truly value satisfying yourself. Working from that place, being in fellowships without an agenda, brings a satisfied excitement; that, today, is fun.

A while back, Diana Nyad, a sixty-four-year-old woman, after two decades of trying, swam from Cuba to America. At her same age, my mother lost her battle with breast cancer. Life is unpredictable and has very different plans for all of us. There will be heroism and tragedy; each new day has the promise of both. Learning to live in (and accept) that dichotomy provides the adrenaline to always move ahead and be grateful for what we have. It can power us all to great things if we recognize it. It can be the source of our greatest possibility, to know and to feel with every level of our own consciousness that we are alive. That this, right here, right now, is our life. It is not our parents' or our children's, not our husbands' or our wives'. It is not made more or less valuable by our job or how much we have in the bank. Our life is ours. It is the only one we will ever have. And we should love it.

ACKNOWLEDGMENTS

Sheryl: I love you. Thank you for loving me for so long, for accepting me and raising me up, flaws and all.

Matthew and Johnowen, the gifts of my life, for being the beautiful, smart, loving and hilarious young men you are. You make me so proud and I love you both beyond all measure.

Dad: Thank you for your love, lessons and inspiration.

My brothers Chad, Micah and Justin: Thank you for having my back, making me laugh and for giving me such amazing nieces and nephews.

To: Lucas, Jacob, Emmett, Luna, Mabel, Fiona and Jackson. It will be a blessing to watch you carry the torch. You make me a very proud uncle.

To Brian and Jodi: Your love and support are never taken for granted. Thank you.

To Kim and to Marcia: Thank you for being in my life, and for loving your two amazing men. They are lucky to have you.

Tom Barrack: Thanks for your love, friendship, wisdom and all of the adventures, past and future!

Maria Shriver: You and the family mean the world to Sheryl and me. Thanks for being there for us.

Betty Wyman: For so many years of guidance. I'm not here without you.

Olaf and Eva Hermes: You have been so important to my family and have changed our lives. We love you.

Caroline Smith: Thank you for my future.

Carol Andrade: For your love and devotion, and for taking such good care of us for so many years.

Jen Harris: For your loyalty, work ethic and kindness. For multi-tasking my life and typing up my chicken-scratch writing for this book.

Carmen Bautista: For loving my boys, your support of Sheryl and always laughing at my jokes.

Miguel Perez: My warrior on the road. I'm literally not going anywhere without you.

To Lupe, Socorro and JP: Thanks for keeping me fed, happy and caffeinated.

Marc Gurvitz, Richard Weitz, Adam Venit, Alan Nierob, Jon Liebman, Jonathan West, Michele Schweitzer, Esther Chang, Jennifer Rudolph Walsh, Brian DePersia, Mari Cardoos Layne, Craig Szabo, Cathy DeLuca, Mark Morrow, Maribeth Annaguey, Chris Jacobs and Larry Stein: I couldn't ask for more; you lead me with passion, smarts and loyalty. Thank you.

Jan Miller: For the advice, friendship and beautiful hospitality.

To Lisa Crowell: My "photo sleuth." You saved me!

Jonathan Karp: You were one of the first to see what I could do, and it meant more than you know. It's been an honor to attempt to live up to your vision.

Everyone at Simon & Schuster: I deeply appreciate your confidence and hard work on behalf of this book: Richard Rhorer, Nicholas Greene, Anne Tate Pearce, Cary Goldstein, Elina Vaysbeyn, Jackie Seow, Lance Fitzgerald, Joy O'Meara, Lisa Erwin and Irene Kheradi.

To all my friends and colleagues both current and throughout the years: Some of you are mentioned in these pages and some are not, but you *all* have inspired me.

ACKNOWLEDGMENTS

To my fans and friends throughout the world: I never forget that without your support, it all stops. I never take your interest for granted. Thank you.

To my friends in recovery: Thank you for helping the promises come true.

To everyone with passion, hope and a dream.

ABOUT THE AUTHOR

Rob Lowe is a film, television and theater actor; a producer; and an entrepreneur. He is also involved in politics and is the author of *Stories I Only Tell My Friends: An Autobiography*. He lives in Los Angeles.